Porch & Patio
Plastic Canvas™

EDITED BY VICKI BLIZZARD

the Needlecraft Shop

Porch & Patio Plastic Canvas

EDITOR Vicki Blizzard

ART DIRECTOR Brad Snow

PUBLISHING SERVICES MANAGER Brenda Gallmeyer

ASSOCIATE EDITOR Lisa M. Fosnaugh

ASSISTANT ART DIRECTOR Nick Pierce

COPY SUPERVISOR Michelle Beck

COPY EDITORS Nicki Lehman
Joanne Dufault
Mary O'Donnell
Beverly Richardson

TECHNICAL EDITOR June Sprunger

GRAPHIC PRODUCTION SUPERVISOR Ronda Bechinski

GRAPHIC ARTISTS Debby Keel
Edith Teegarden

PRODUCTION ASSISTANTS Cheryl Kempf
Marj Morgan
Judy Neuenschwander

PHOTOGRAPHY Tammy Christian
Don Clark
Matthew Owen
Jackie Schaffel

PHOTO STYLISTS Tammy Nussbaum
Tammy M. Smith

CHIEF EXECUTIVE OFFICER John Robinson

PUBLISHING DIRECTOR David McKee

MARKETING DIRECTOR Dan Fink

Printed in the China
First Printing: 2006
Library of Congress Control Number: 2005938068
Hardcover ISBN: 1-57367-215-7
Softcover ISBN: 1-57367-241-6

1 2 3 4 5 6 7 8 9

Welcome!

Don't you just love adding unexpected decorating touches to your home? A glass tube attached to a window to hold a colorful bloom, a jar of beads or buttons sitting on a shelf, a treasured ornament hanging from the center of a chandelier—all of these are unexpected, but they add so much to the overall look of a room.

I really like to add the unexpected to my outside "rooms." I have interesting little statues hidden throughout my vegetable and flower gardens. I place candles all over the back porch when I'm having dinner outside in the evening. And of course I have wind chimes wherever the breeze will blow through them—inside, on the front porch, and even in the trees behind my home.

The designs in this book are all suitable for decorating your own outside rooms. Placed in sunrooms or on protected patios and porches, these projects will add unexpected whimsy and fun to greet your guests as they arrive at your front door and to make you smile as you're watering your potted plants. And, yes, there are wind chimes galore to entertain several of your senses.

We enjoyed imagining how these projects would look in our homes, and we know you'll enjoy stitching them for yours.

Have fun!

Vicki Blizzard

Plant Accessories

Suncatchers

Tissue Box Covers

Welcome Signs & Door Decor

Wind Chimes, Spinners & Mobiles

Table Decor

Plant Accessories

No matter how your garden grows, you'll love these fun and fabulous accessories for your plants. From pot covers to funky pokes, there's something for everyone.

Pot Overalls

Not meant to get grubby, these overalls are sized just right for a 4-inch pot with saucer. DESIGN BY RONDA BRYCE

Skill Level

Intermediate

Size

4¼ inches W x 7¼ inches H x 4¼ inches D (10.8cm x 18.4cm x 10.8cm)

Materials

- 1 sheet 7-count plastic canvas
- 1 (4-inch) Uniek Quick-Shape plastic canvas radial circle
- 2 (3-inch) Uniek Quick-Shape plastic canvas radial circles
- Uniek Needloft plastic canvas yarn as listed in color key
- #16 tapestry needle
- 2 (¾-inch/1.9cm) hook-and-loop coins
- 2 (¾-inch/1.9cm) pink buttons
- Small yellow butterfly button
- Hand-sewing needle
- White, pink and blue sewing thread

Overalls

1. Cut overalls from 7-count plastic canvas according to graphs (page 10).

2. Stitch overalls; Overcast top edges from dot to dot.

3. Whipstitch side edges together, forming back seam, then Whipstitch bottom edge to unstitched 4-inch radial circle.

Legs

1. Cut and stitch legs from 7-count plastic canvas according to graphs (page 10).

2. For leg base pieces, cut the three outermost rows of holes from two 3-inch radial circles. Do not stitch.

3. Using sail blue through step 4, fold each leg in a cylinder and Whipstitch 11-hole edges together. Whipstitch bottom edge of each leg to one base; Overcast top edges.

4. Placing seams in back, tack top edges of legs to bottom of 4-inch radial circle.

Straps & Patches

1. Cut straps and patches from 7-count plastic canvas according to graphs (page 10).

2. Stitch and Overcast pieces following graphs.

3. Using hand-sewing needle through step 4, use pink thread to stitch buttons to front of straps where indicated with pink shading.

4. Using white thread, stitch hook-and-loop coins to front of overall bib where indicated with yellow shading and to back of straps behind buttons.

5. Using sail blue, tack other ends of straps to inside back of overalls where indicated on graph with blue shading.

6. Using photo as a guide through step 7, use hand-sewing needle and white thread to attach patches to front of overalls.

7. Using hand-sewing needle and blue thread, attach yellow butterfly button to strap. 🍃

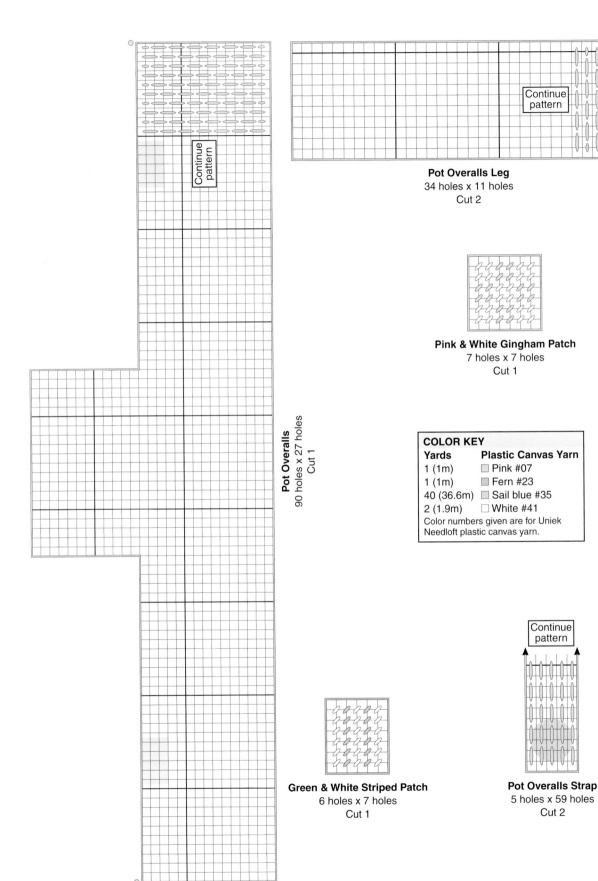

Pot Overalls Leg
34 holes x 11 holes
Cut 2

Pink & White Gingham Patch
7 holes x 7 holes
Cut 1

Continue pattern

Pot Overalls
90 holes x 27 holes
Cut 1

Continue pattern

COLOR KEY	
Yards	**Plastic Canvas Yarn**
1 (1m)	Pink #07
1 (1m)	Fern #23
40 (36.6m)	Sail blue #35
2 (1.9m)	White #41

Color numbers given are for Uniek Needloft plastic canvas yarn.

Green & White Striped Patch
6 holes x 7 holes
Cut 1

Continue pattern

Pot Overalls Strap
5 holes x 59 holes
Cut 2

Flowerpot Cover

Display a potted plant in style with a stitched hanging plant cover that imitates the look of macramé. DESIGN BY HEATHE SCHUTZE

Skill Level
Intermediate

Size
Approximately 6½ inches H x 7¾ inches in diameter (16.5cm x 19.7cm), excluding braided hanger

Materials
- 3 regular-size sheets clear 7-count plastic canvas
- 1 regular-size sheet light green 7-count plastic canvas
- Worsted weight yarn as listed in color key
- DMC 6-strand variegated embroidery floss as listed in color key
- #16 tapestry needle
- Hot-glue gun

Cutting & Stitching
1. Cut outer sides, joining flowers and base from clear plastic canvas according to graphs (pages 12, 13, 14 and 15). Base will remain unstitched.

2. Cut inner sides and braid braces from light green plastic canvas according to graphs (page 14).

3. Stitch outer side pieces following graphs, working uncoded areas on flowers with lilac Continental

Stitches and leaving shaded yellow areas unstitched at this time.

4. Matching edges, put ends with half flowers together. Place single joining flower over half flower pieces, then stitch flower through both layers. Whipstitch edges of medium sage bands together above and below flower with Continental Stitches.

5. Place remaining ends together, matching edges and forming a circle. Center double joining flowers over two unstitched flowers on outer side, then stitch flowers through both layers. Whip-stitch edges of bands together above and below flowers with Continental Stitches.

6. When background stitching is completed, Overcast all edges. Use variegated floss to work Backstitches and Straight Stitches on flowers.

7. Using medium sage through step 8, overlap two rows of holes of inner sides A and B, then Continental Stitch together as shown on graph. Repeat with remaining ends, forming a circle.

8. Whipstitch bottom edge of inner side to base, easing as necessary to fit.

Braided Hanger

1. Cut nine (78-inch/2m) lengths of medium sage yarn. Place lengths together and fold in half. Tie a knot in folded end, making a 3-inch (7.6cm) loop. Divide yarn below knot into three groups of six and braid until 24 inches (61cm) long. Secure end of braid temporarily.

2. Cut 27 (2-yard/1.9m) lengths of medium sage yarn. Place in three groups of nine lengths. Thread one length through hole between knot and braid (see Fig. 1) of first group to half-way point. Braid until 24 (61cm) inches long. Secure end temporarily.

3. Repeat step 2 with remaining two groups of yarn.

4. Thread four braids from top to bottom through four holes in base. Make sure braids are pulled through so basket hangs straight, then release ends and tie together in a knot under base forming a tassel. Trim tassel to about 2 inches (5.1cm).

Final Assembly

1. Overlapping two holes at ends, place braid braces along top edge of inner side so braids are between braces and inner side.

2. Keeping braids evenly spaced, Continental Stitch braces and inner side together, passing over braided areas.

3. Slide outer side over inner side until top and bottom edges of inner side are even with edges on top and bottom bands of outer side. Glue in place. 🍃

COLOR KEY

Yards	Worsted Weight Yarn
100 (91.5m)	▨ Medium sage
3 (2.8m)	☐ Medium yellow
30 (27.5m)	Uncoded areas on flowers are lilac Continental Stitches
	⁄ Lilac Overcasting
	6-Strand Embroidery Floss
8 (7.4m)	⁄ Variegated violet #52 Backstitch and Straight Stitch

Color number given is for DMC 6-strand embroidery floss.

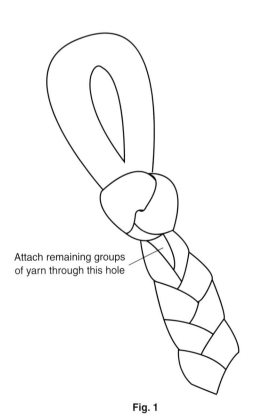

Attach remaining groups of yarn through this hole

Fig. 1

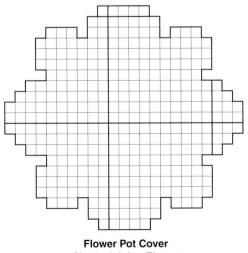

Flower Pot Cover
Single Joining Flower
23 holes x 21 holes
Cut 1 from clear

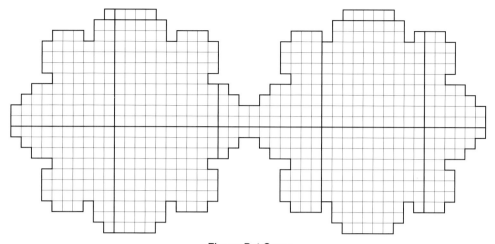

Flower Pot Cover
Double Joining Flowers
46 holes x 21 holes
Cut 1 from clear

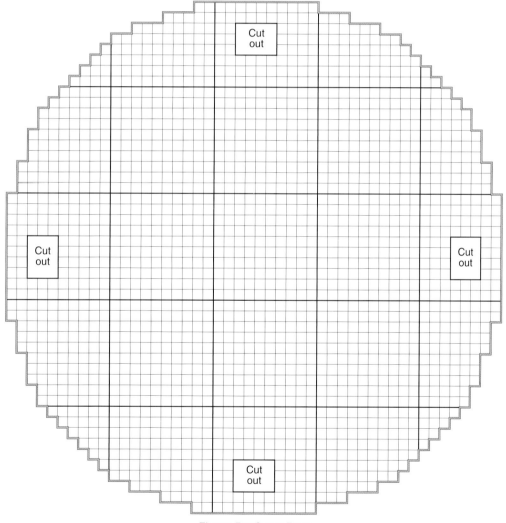

Cut
out

Cut
out

Cut
out

Cut
out

Flower Pot Cover Base
48 holes x 48 holes
Cut 1 from clear
Do not stitch

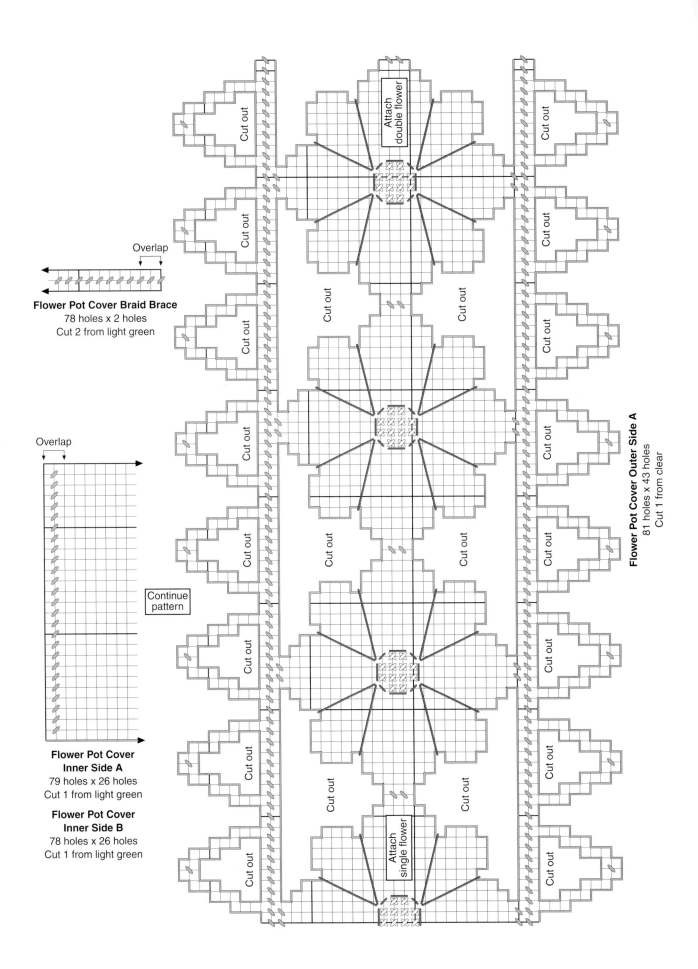

Flower Pot Cover Braid Brace
78 holes x 2 holes
Cut 2 from light green

Overlap

Overlap

Continue
pattern

**Flower Pot Cover
Inner Side A**
79 holes x 26 holes
Cut 1 from light green

**Flower Pot Cover
Inner Side B**
78 holes x 26 holes
Cut 1 from light green

Attach
double flower

Attach
single flower

Cut out

Flower Pot Cover Outer Side A
81 holes x 43 holes
Cut 1 from clear

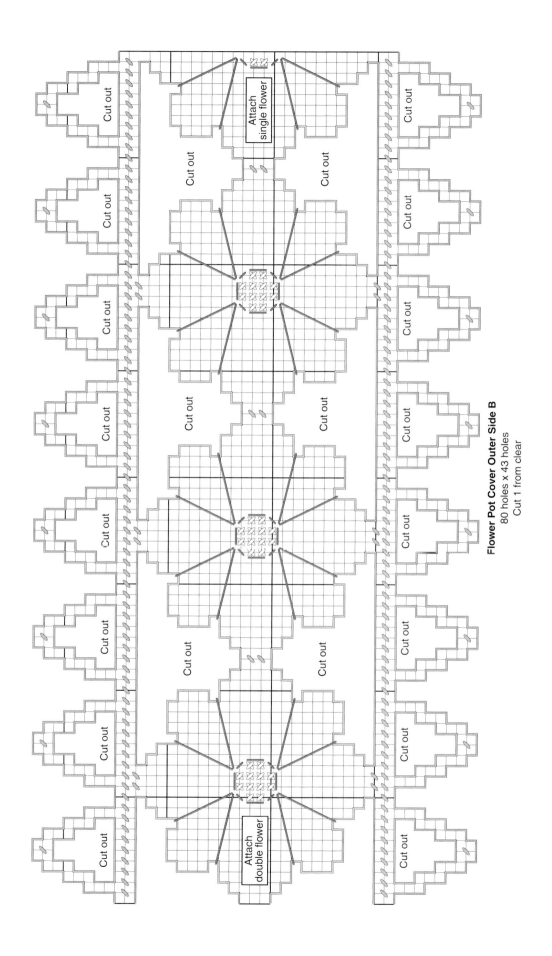

Flower Pot Cover Outer Side B
80 holes x 43 holes
Cut 1 from clear

Attach single flower

Attach double flower

Cut out

Whimsical Plant Pokes

Combine beads, metallic cord and novelty yarn along with worsted weight yarn to create one-of-a-kind pokes in a variety of motifs. DESIGNS BY GINA WOODS

Skill Level
Beginner

Size
Bird's Nest: 5⅝ inches W x 3⅝ inches H (14.3cm x 9.2cm), excluding poke

Butterfly: 3⅝ inches W x 2¾ inches H (9.2cm x 7cm), excluding poke

Dragonflies: 4 inches W x 3½ inches H (10.2cm x 8.9cm), excluding poke

Snail: 3⅝ inches W x 4¼ inches H (9.2cm x 10.8cm), excluding poke

Watering Can: 5½ inches W x 2⅝ inches H (14cm x 6cm), excluding poke

Materials
Each
- Small amount 7-count plastic canvas
- Worsted weight yarn as listed in color key
- #16 tapestry needle
- 8 inches (20.3cm) 20-gauge copper and/or gold wire
- Large felt-tip marker

Bird's Nest
- Small amount 7-count plastic canvas
- 1½ yards (1.4m) Patons Yarn Allure mink #04013 super bulky eyelash yarn from Spinrite Inc.
- Hot-glue gun

Butterfly
- 6-strand embroidery floss as listed in color key
- 2 round purple pearl-headed pins
- Hot-glue gun

Dragonfly
- Metallic craft cord as listed in color key
- Faceted beads in colors desired:
  - 5 (4mm)
  - 4 (6mm)
  - 3 (8mm)
- 2 round pearl-headed pins in desired color
- Hand-sewing needle
- Thread to match beads or body color
- Hot-glue gun

Snail
- 6-strand embroidery floss as listed in color key
- 1½-inches (3.8cm) white iridescent chenille stem
- 5mm red pompom
- 2 round green pearl-headed pins
- Hot-glue gun

Watering Can
- Metallic craft cord as listed in color key
- Solid metallic craft cord as listed in color key
- 6-strand embroidery floss as listed in color key

Project Note
Samples show a variety of four dragonflies. Instructions and yardage are for one dragonfly.

Bird's Nest
1. Cut plastic canvas according to graphs (page 39).

2. Overcast branch then work Straight Stitch. Stitch and Overcast nest back, eggs and leaves following graphs working one large leaf and one small leaf with clover green and two large leaves and one small leaf with yellow green.

3. For nest front, cut a 1½ yard (1.4m) length of mink eyelash yarn. Thread 12 inches (30.5cm) down through hole indicated with red dot.

4. Leaving this tail hanging for the moment, take remaining yarn up to point A and begin wrapping yarn snugly around nest to point B, covering all canvas on this side of nest. Glue end to back; trim as needed.

5. Wrap remaining section of nest front with the 12-inch (30.5cm)

length until canvas is covered. Glue end to back; trim as needed.

6. Using photo as a guide through step 8, glue eggs in a cluster to center top of nest back. Place a line of glue on nest back where indicated with blue line, then glue wrong side of nest front in place so that top of nest just covers bottom of eggs.

7. Glue branch behind assembled nest, then glue leaves to branch and nest.

8. Wrap center of copper wire around marker to make three or four coils. Pull wire to loosen coils. Trim top of wire to extend 2 inches (5.1cm) above coils, then slide under stitching at center back of nest. Trim bottom end as desired.

Butterfly

1. Cut plastic canvas according to graphs (page 39).

2. Overcast body then work Straight Stitch down center. Stitch and Overcast wings following graph, working uncoded areas with dark aqua Continental Stitches.

3. When background stitching is completed, work black floss embroidery on wings.

4. For antennae, push pins into stitching on top back of body. Glue body to center of wings.

5. Wrap center of copper wire around marker. Pull wire to loosen coils. Trim top of wire to extend 2 inches (5.1cm) above coils, then slide under several stitches at center back wings. Trim bottom end as desired.

Dragonfly

1. Cut plastic canvas according to graphs (page 19).

2. Stitch and Overcast pieces following graphs, working body/tail with worsted weight yarn and wings with metallic craft cord.

3. When background stitching is completed, use hand-sewing needle and thread to attach beads

Watering Can

1. Cut plastic canvas according to graph (page 19).

2. Stitch and Overcast piece following graph, working uncoded background with light yellow Continental Stitches.

3. When background stitching and Overcasting are completed, work Backstitches, Straight Stitches, Lazy Daisy Stitches and French Knots with 6-strand embroidery floss, wrapping French Knots two times.

4. Using photo as a guide, secure two lengths turquoise metallic craft cord behind stitching on sprinkler, leaving about 2-inch (5.1cm) tails. Fray ends of cord to imitate sprinkling water.

5. Wrap center of copper wire around marker to make three or four coils. Pull wire to loosen coils. Trim top of wire to extend 2 inches (5.1cm) above coils, then slide under stitching at bottom left corner of can so can looks like it is tipping and water is sprinkling out of the spout. Trim bottom end of wire as desired. ✍

to body and tail where indicated on graph.

4. For antennae, push pins into stitching on top back of body.

5. Using photo as a guide, glue wings to back of body.

6. Wrap center of copper wire around marker to make three or four coils. Pull wire to loosen coils. Trim top of wire to extend 2 inches (5.1cm) above coils, then slide under stitching at center back of body. Trim bottom end as desired.

Snail

1. Cut plastic canvas according to graphs (page 19).

2. Overcast door roof with medium copper. Stitch and Overcast remaining pieces following graphs, working uncoded background on shell with very pale green Continental Stitches.

3. When background stitching is completed, use 2 plies each medium and light spring green to work spiral embroidery on shell. Work all remaining embroidery on shell and body with black floss, wrapping French Knots two times.

4. For antennae, push pins into stitching on top back of head where indicated on graph with

arrows. Curl one end of chenille stem. Glue other end behind center top of chimney.

5. Using photo as a guide, glue as follows: shell to body, door roof to shell over door, chimney behind shell and red pompom to head for nose.

6. Wrap center of copper wire around marker to make three or four coils. Pull wire to loosen coils. Trim top of wire to extend 2 inches (5.1cm) above coils, then slide under stitching at center back of shell. Trim bottom end as desired.

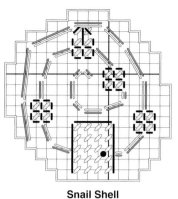

Snail Shell
16 holes x 16 holes
Cut 1

Snail Chimney
4 holes x 8 holes
Cut 1

Snail Door Roof
4 holes x 4 holes
Cut 1

COLOR KEY
SNAIL

Yards	Worsted Weight Yarn
5 (4.6m)	Medium spring green
4 (3.7m)	Light spring green
2 (1.9m)	Medium copper
2 (1.9m)	Light terra-cotta
2 (1.9m)	Aqua
5 (4.6m)	Uncoded background on shell is very pale green Continental Stitches
	∕ Medium spring green (2-ply) Straight Stitch and Backstitch
	∕ Light spring green (2-ply) Straight Stitch and Backstitch
	6-Strand Embroidery Floss
2 (1.9m)	∕ Black Backstitch
	● Black (2-wrap) French Knot
	● Attach red pompom

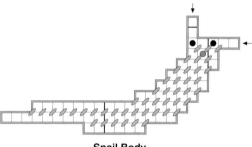

Snail Body
23 holes x 11 holes
Cut 1

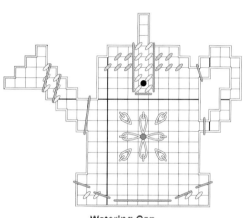

Watering Can
23 holes x 18 holes
Cut 1

Glue this
end to body →

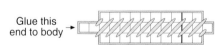

Dragonfly Wing
13 holes x 3 holes
Cut 4

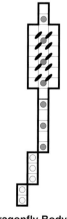

Dragonfly Body/Tail
4 holes x 19 holes
Cut 1

COLOR KEY
DRAGONFLY

Yards	Worsted Weight Yarn
2 (1.9m)	■ Body color of choice
	Metallic Craft Cord
4 (3.7m)	□ Wings color of choice
	○ Attach 4mm bead
	● Attach 6mm bead
	● Attach 8mm bead

COLOR KEY
WATERING CAN

Yards	Worsted Weight Yarn
2 (1.9m)	□ Gold
5 (4.6m)	Uncoded background is light yellow Continental Stitches
	∕ Light yellow Overcasting
	Metallic Craft Cord
1 (1m)	□ Turquoise
	Solid Metallic Craft Cord
1 (1m)	∕ Solid silver Overcasting
	6-Strand Embroidery Floss
2 (1.9m)	∕ Dark gold Backstitch and Straight Stitch
1 (1m)	⊘ Dark pink Lazy Daisy Stitch
1 (1m)	⊘ Light green Lazy Daisy Stitch
1 (1m)	● Red (2-wrap) French Knot
1 (1m)	● Black (2-wrap) French Knot

Graphs continued on page 39

Critter Planters

Grow tiny herbs and spices in these delightful garden creatures. DESIGNS BY CAROLE RODGERS

Skill Level

Intermediate

Size

Camel: 8¼ inches L x 4¾ inches H x 3⅜ inches D (21cm x 14cm x 8.6cm)

Caterpillar: 8¾ inches L x 2½ inches H x 2⅜ inches D (22.2cm x 6.4cm x 6cm)

Frog: 2¾ inches W x 4 inches H x 3 inches D (7cm x 10.2cm x 7.6cm)

Ladybug: 6⅞ inches L x 3 inches H x 5⅛ inches D (17.5cm x 7.6cm x 13cm), excluding legs

Snail: 2⅞ inches W x 8¾ inches L x 5½ inches H (7.3cm x 22.2cm x 14cm)

Turtle: 6 inches W x 9 inches L x 2¼ inches H (15.2cm x 23.5cm x 14cm)

Materials

Each

- Uniek Needloft plastic canvas yarn as listed in color key
- #16 tapestry needle
- Fabric glue

Camel

- 2 sheets 7-count stiff plastic canvas
- 2 (2¼-inch/5.7cm) terra-cotta pots

Caterpillar

- 1 sheet 7-count stiff plastic canvas
- 3 (1½-inch/3.8cm) terra-cotta pots
- Black chenille stem
- 10mm black pompom

Frog

- 1 sheet 7-count regular plastic canvas
- 3-inch Uniek QuickShape plastic canvas radial circle
- 2½-inch (6.4cm) terra-cotta pot

Ladybug

- 1 sheet 7-count regular plastic canvas
- 2 (1½-inch/3.8cm) terra-cotta pots
- 3 black chenille stems
- Black paint
- Small paintbrush

Snail

- 1 sheet 7-count stiff plastic canvas
- 2 (3-inch) Uniek QuickShape plastic canvas radial circles
- 3-inch (7.6cm) terra-cotta pot
- 6 inches (15.2cm) black chenille stem

Turtle

- 1 sheet 7-count stiff plastic canvas
- 4-inch Uniek QuickShape plastic canvas radial circle
- 4-inch (10.2cm) terra-cotta saucer

Camel

1. Cut plastic canvas according to graphs (pages 24 and 25).

2. Stitch and Overcast legs following graph, reversing one before stitching.

3. Stitch remaining pieces following graphs, reversing one head/neck. Overcast inside edges on back.

4. Whipstitch side edges of rump to sides, then Whipstitch head/neck to sides.

5. Thread three 8-inch/20.3cm-lengths of camel yarn through holes indicated on rump graph; secure on backside. Braid until 1½ inches/3.8cm long, then tie with another length camel yarn. Cut tip of tail to ¾ inches; fluff with needle.

6. Whipstitch camel back to rump, sides and head/neck, attaching back edges to rump from blue dot to blue dot and front edges to head/neck from red dot to red dot.

7. Whipstitch head edges together from arrow to arrow. Whipstitch underbelly to rump, sides and head/neck, attaching back edges to rump from blue dot to blue dot and front edges to head/neck from red dot to red dot.

8. Center and glue legs to sides, covering unstitched areas on sides.

9. Place terra-cotta pots in holes.

Caterpillar

1. Cut plastic canvas according to graphs (page 23). Cut three 12-hole x 12-hole pieces for pot holder base pieces. Pot holder side and base pieces will remain unstitched.

2. Stitch one caterpillar piece as graphed. Reverse remaining caterpillar piece and stitch with reverse Slanted Gobelin Stitches.

3. Overcast top and bottom edges of caterpillars from dot to dot, leaving nose and tail edges unworked at this time. Work black Backstitches for mouth.

4. Whipstitch wrong sides of nose edges together; Whipstitch tail edges together.

5. Stitch pot holder top and end pieces following graphs.

6. Using fern throughout, Whipstitch top pieces to top edges of sides from arrow to arrow. Repeat with base pieces, Whipstitching to bottom edges of sides. Whipstitch ends to top, side and base pieces. Do not Overcast remaining edges.

7. Glue assembled pot holder inside caterpillar where indicated with yellow shading.

8. For antennae, cut two 4-inch (10.2cm) lengths from black chenille stem. Curl one end on each; glue other ends behind head where indicated on graph. For nose, glue pompom to front edge where indicated.

9. Place terra-cotta pots in holes.

Frog

1. Cut plastic canvas according to graphs (page 24). For base, cut the outermost row of holes from 3-inch radial circle. Base will remain unstitched.

2. Stitch and Overcast head and legs, working uncoded

areas on head with holly Continental Stitches.

3. When background stitching is completed, work white French Knots in middle of eyes.

4. Stitch body following graph. Using holly, Whipstitch side edges together, then Whipstitch bottom edges to unstitched base. Overcast top edges with holly, forest and fern as graphed.

5. Using photo as guide throughout, glue legs to body front, making sure bottom edges of front and legs are even. Center head over top of legs; glue in place.

6. Place terra-cotta pot in frog body.

Ladybug

1. Cut plastic canvas according to graphs (page 27).

2. Stitch wings, head top, head side, body sides and tail following graphs. Underbelly will remain unstitched.

3. Using black, Overcast inside edges of wings; Whipstitch wing pieces together along top edges from dot to dot. Overcast remaining edges with red.

4. Following ladybug assembly diagram (page 27), Whipstitch body sides to tail. Matching bottom edges, Whipstitch body side to head side. *Note: Head side is two holes shorter than body sides.*

5. Whipstitch head side to head top. Whipstitch tail, body sides and head side to unstitched underbelly.

6. Place glue on top edges of body; center wings on top and press into glue. Hold until glue sets.

7. For legs, cut six 4-inch (10.2cm) lengths of black chenille stem. Fold each in the middle. Glue ends of three to each body side, making sure to glue just under wings (see

photo). Shape legs as desired.

8. For antennae, cut two 4-inch (10.2cm) lengths of black chenille stem. Curl one end on each, making ½-inch (1.3cm) curls. Glue other ends to top front of head where indicated on graph. Bend each antenna slightly.

9. Paint terra-cotta pots with black; allow to dry. Place pots in holes on wings.

Snail

1. Cut snails from plastic canvas according to graph (page 26). Cut one 60-hole x 13-hole piece for pot stand side. Pot stand side will remain unstitched.

2. Stitch one snail following graph. Reverse remaining snail before stitching.

3. Overcast top edges of shells from dot to dot and bottom edges of snail bodies from arrow to arrow. Whipstitch wrong sides of snails together along remaining edges.

4. Using brown, Whipstitch 13-hole edges of pot stand together forming a cylinder, then Whipstitch one 3-inch unstitched radial circle each to top and bottom edges.

5. Place glue on stitching on assembled pot stand, then slide snail body over stand until bottom edges are even. Allow to dry.

6. For antennae, thread chenille stem through hole indicated on snail head to center of stem. Curl ends (see photo).

7. Place terra-cotta pot on stand in snail shell.

Turtle

1. Cut pieces from plastic canvas according to graphs (page 26).

2. Stitch one head, one tail and two feet following graphs. Reverse remaining head and tail; stitch with

Slanted Gobelin and Continental Stitches. Reverse remaining feet; stitch with Reverse Slanted Gobelin Stitches.

3. Stitch body following graph. Whipstitch short ends of body pieces together along short edges with black. Whipstitch bottom edge to 4-inch radial circle with yellow.

4. Using fern through step 6, Overcast around side and bottom edges of feet. Overcast top edge of body, Whipstitching top edges of feet to top edge of body where indicated while Overcasting.

5. Overcast around neck edges of head pieces from dot to dot, then Whipstitch wrong sides together along remaining edges. Separate neck edges at bottom; glue to front of body over seam (see photo).

6. Overcast front edges of tail pieces from dot to dot, then Whipstitch wrong sides together along remaining edges. Separate front edges and glue to back of body where indicated.

7. Place terra-cotta saucer in body.

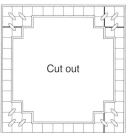

Caterpillar Planter Holder Top
12 holes x 12 holes
Cut 3 from stiff

Caterpillar Planter Holder End
12 holes x 12 holes
Cut 2 from stiff

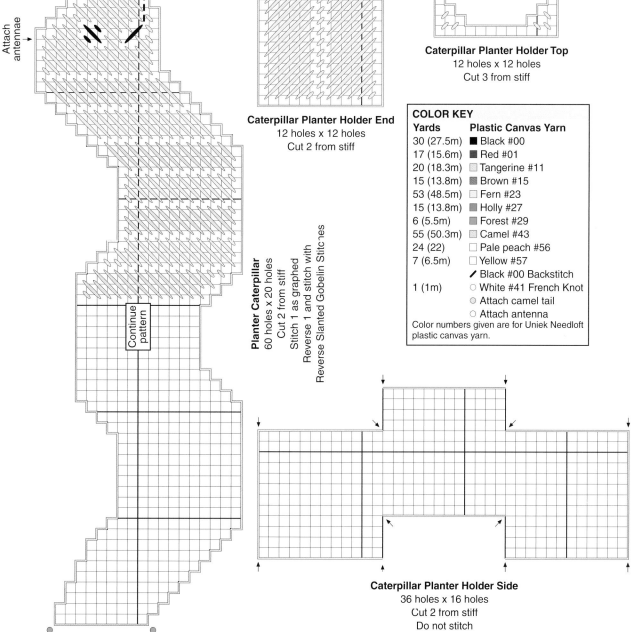

Attach pompom

Attach antennae

Continue pattern

Planter Caterpillar
60 holes x 20 holes
Cut 2 from stiff
Stitch 1 as graphed
Reverse 1 and stitch with
Reverse Slanted Gobelin Stitches

COLOR KEY

Yards		Plastic Canvas Yarn
30 (27.5m)	■	Black #00
17 (15.6m)	■	Red #01
20 (18.3m)	□	Tangerine #11
15 (13.8m)	▨	Brown #15
53 (48.5m)	□	Fern #23
15 (13.8m)	▨	Holly #27
6 (5.5m)	▨	Forest #29
55 (50.3m)	□	Camel #43
24 (22)	□	Pale peach #56
7 (6.5m)	□	Yellow #57
1 (1m)	✦	Black #00 Backstitch
	○	White #41 French Knot
	○	Attach camel tail
	○	Attach antenna

Color numbers given are for Uniek Needloft plastic canvas yarn.

Caterpillar Planter Holder Side
36 holes x 16 holes
Cut 2 from stiff
Do not stitch

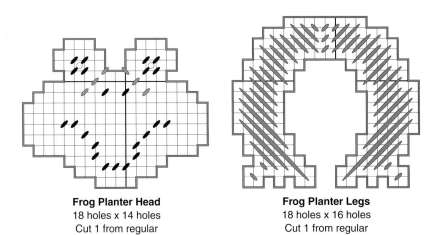

Frog Planter Head
18 holes x 14 holes
Cut 1 from regular

Frog Planter Legs
18 holes x 16 holes
Cut 1 from regular

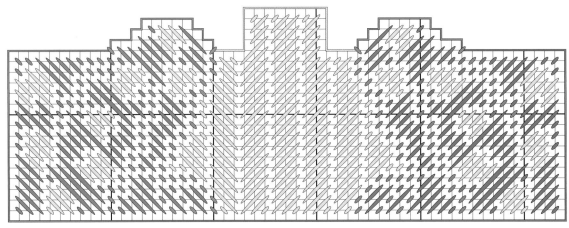

Frog Planter Body
54 holes x 20 holes
Cut 1 from regular

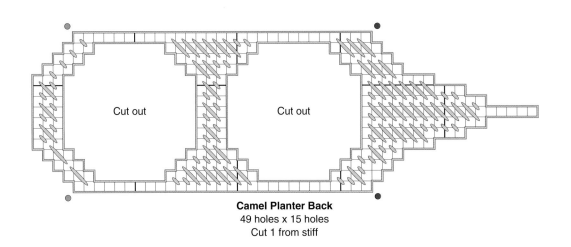

Cut out

Cut out

Camel Planter Back
49 holes x 15 holes
Cut 1 from stiff

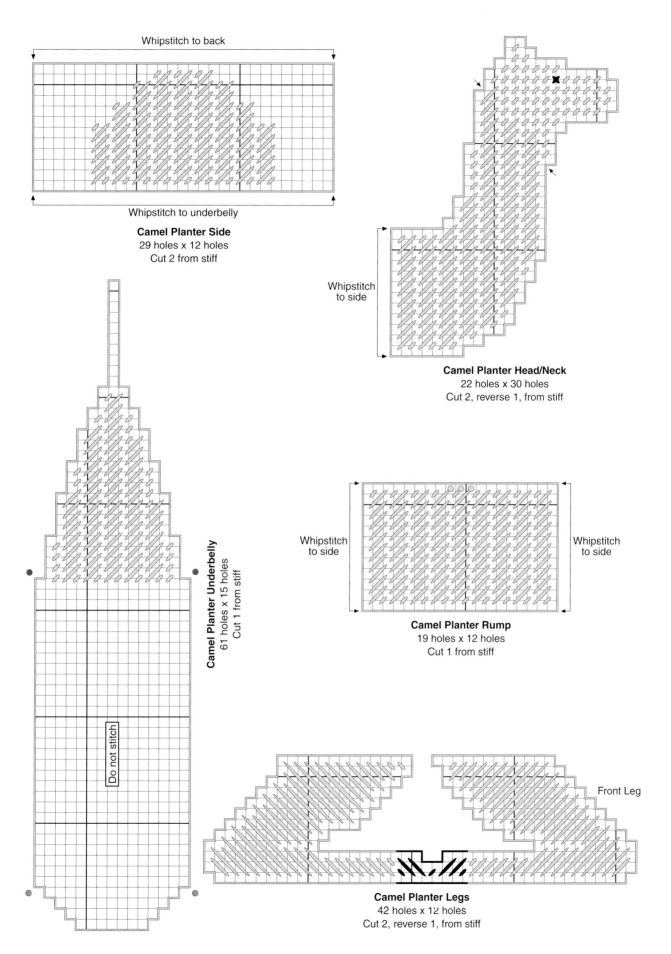

Whipstitch to back

Whipstitch to underbelly

Camel Planter Side
29 holes x 12 holes
Cut 2 from stiff

Whipstitch
to side

Camel Planter Head/Neck
22 holes x 30 holes
Cut 2, reverse 1, from stiff

Camel Planter Underbelly
61 holes x 15 holes
Cut 1 from stiff

Do not stitch

Whipstitch
to side

Whipstitch
to side

Camel Planter Rump
19 holes x 12 holes
Cut 1 from stiff

Front Leg

Camel Planter Legs
42 holes x 12 holes
Cut 2, reverse 1, from stiff

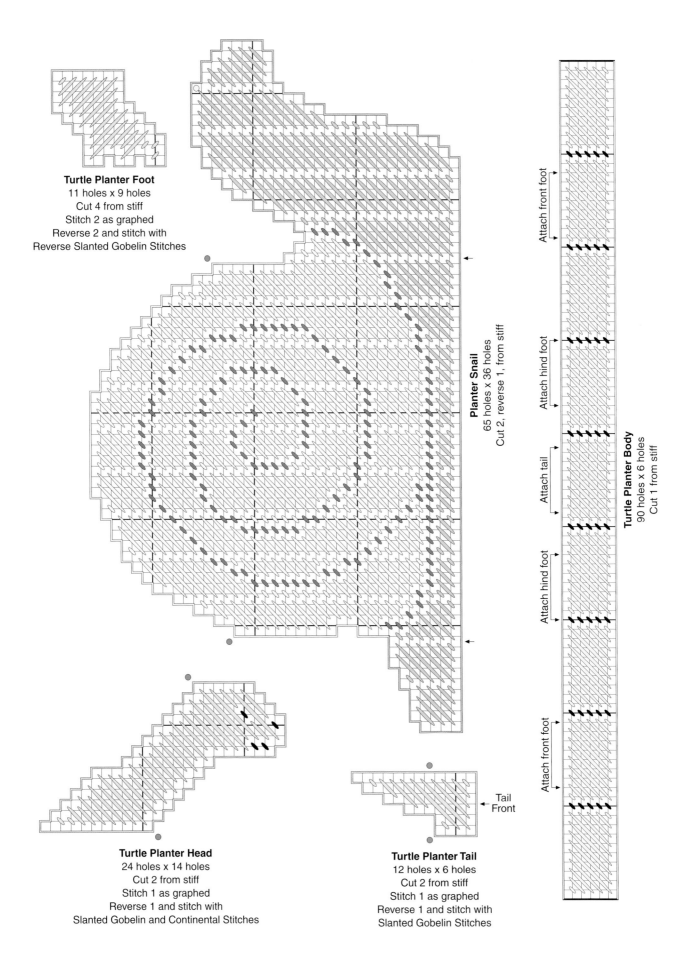

Turtle Planter Foot
11 holes x 9 holes
Cut 4 from stiff
Stitch 2 as graphed
Reverse 2 and stitch with
Reverse Slanted Gobelin Stitches

Planter Snail
65 holes x 36 holes
Cut 2, reverse 1, from stiff

Turtle Planter Body
90 holes x 6 holes
Cut 1 from stiff

Attach front foot

Attach hind foot

Attach tail

Attach hind foot

Attach front foot

Turtle Planter Head
24 holes x 14 holes
Cut 2 from stiff
Stitch 1 as graphed
Reverse 1 and stitch with
Slanted Gobelin and Continental Stitches

Turtle Planter Tail
12 holes x 6 holes
Cut 2 from stiff
Stitch 1 as graphed
Reverse 1 and stitch with
Slanted Gobelin Stitches

Tail
Front

COLOR KEY

Yards	Plastic Canvas Yarn
30 (27.5m)	■ Black #00
17 (15.6m)	■ Red #01
20 (18.3m)	□ Tangerine #11
15 (13.8m)	■ Brown #15
53 (48.5m)	□ Fern #23
15 (13.8m)	■ Holly #27
6 (5.5m)	■ Forest #29
55 (50.3m)	□ Camel #43
24 (22)	□ Pale peach #56
7 (6.5m)	□ Yellow #57
	✦ Black #00 Backstitch
1 (1m)	○ White #41 French Knot
	◎ Attach camel tail
	◎ Attach antenna

Color numbers given are for Uniek Needloft plastic canvas yarn.

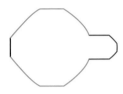

Ladybug Planter Assembly Diagram
Tail = black line
Body sides = blue lines
Head side = red line

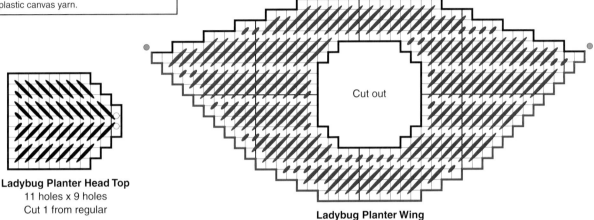

Ladybug Planter Wing
42 holes x 19 holes
Cut 2 from regular

Ladybug Planter Head Top
11 holes x 9 holes
Cut 1 from regular

Continue pattern

Ladybug Planter Head Side
27 holes x 4 holes
Cut 1 from regular

Ladybug Planter Tail
7 holes x 6 holes
Cut 1 from regular

Ladybug Planter Underbelly
41 holes x 29 holes
Cut 1 from regular
Do not stitch

Continue pattern

Ladybug Planter Body Side
39 holes x 6 holes
Cut 2 from regular

Plant Poke Trio

Themed in classic gardening motifs, this trio will be right at home in a large potted plant. DESIGNS BY PAM BULL

Skill Level

Beginner

Size

Caterpillar: 4¾ inches W x 3⅛ inches H (12.1cm x 8cm), excluding poke
Flower Pot: 3 inches W x 5⅜ inches H (7.6cm x 13.7cm), excluding poke
Ladybug: 4⅛ inches W x 5¼ inches H (10.5cm x 13.3cm), excluding poke

Materials

All
- ⅓ sheet 7-count plastic canvas
- #16 tapestry needle
- Hot-glue gun

Caterpillar
- Uniek Needloft yarn as listed in color key
- Lion Brand Yarn Co. Lion Suede bulky weight yarn as listed in color key
- 2 (8mm) movable eyes
- ¼-inch (0.6cm) white button
- 2½ inches (6.4cm) orange chenille stem
- Several (6–12-inch/15.2–30.5cm) lengths 22-gauge green wire
- 4½-inch (11.4cm) long ³⁄₁₆-inch (0.5cm) wooden dowel

Flower Pot
- Uniek Needloft yarn as listed in color key
- Worsted weight yarn as listed in color key
- Lion Brand Yarn Co. Lion Suede bulky weight yarn as listed in color key
- ½-inch (1.3cm) pink button
- Several (6–12-inch/15.2–30.5cm) lengths 22-gauge green wire
- 13½-inch (34.3cm) length ³⁄₁₆-inch (0.5cm) wooden dowel

Ladybug
- Worsted weight yarn as listed in color key
- Lion Brand Yarn Co., Lion Chenille yarn as listed in color key
- 2 (12mm) movable eyes
- 12 (8mm) black sequins
- 12 (4mm) round black cabochons
- 3½ inches (8.9cm) black chenille stem
- ½-inch (1.3cm) silver button
- Short length twine
- 4 (6–12-inch/15.2–30.5cm) lengths 22-gauge green wire
- 10-inch (25.4cm) long ³⁄₁₆-inch (0.5cm) wooden dowel

Caterpillar

1. Cut caterpillar from plastic canvas according to graph (page 30).
2. Stitch and Overcast piece following graph.
3. Using photo as a guide through step 7, glue movable eyes to head. Cut orange chenille stem in half and bend down one end on each length. Glue to back of head for antennae.
4. Tie a short length of baby blue yarn in a bow and glue to neck of caterpillar. Glue white button to center of bow.
5. For grass, curl lengths of green wire around dowel, then glue as desired to caterpillar.
6. Glue dowel to back of caterpillar.

Flower Pot

1. Cut pot, rim, tulip, stem and leaves from plastic canvas according to graphs (page 30).
2. Stitch and Overcast pieces following graphs. **Note:** *Edges on pot covered by rim are not Overcast.*
3. Using photo as a guide through step 6, glue rim to top front of pot. Center and glue one end of stem to back of pot and other end to center back of tulip. Glue one leaf to back of stem and one to front of stem.
4. Curl lengths of green wire around dowel, then glue as desired around top of pot.

5. Thread desired length of lavender yarn from front to back through holes on pink button; tie in a knot. Glue button to right side of rim.

6. Center and glue dowel to back of pot.

Ladybug

1. Cut ladybug from plastic canvas according to graph.

2. Stitch and Overcast piece following graph, working black Straight Stitches when background stitching is completed.

3. Using photo as a guide through step 7, thread twine from front to back through holes on silver button; tie in a knot. Glue button to bottom right side of body.

4. Glue movable eyes to head. Bend black chenille stem in a "U" shape and glue to back of head for antennae.

5. Glue dowel to center back at bottom of ladybug.

6. Curl lengths of green wire around dowel, then glue two each to bottom of ladybug on both sides of dowel.

7. Glue six sequins as desired to each wing, then glue one cabochon to center of each sequin. 🪶

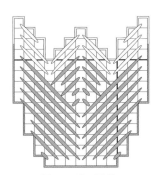

Flower Pot Tulip
13 holes x 14 holes
Cut 1

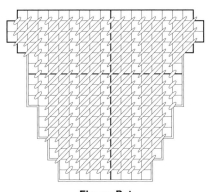

Flower Pot
19 holes x 16 holes
Cut 1

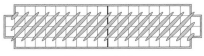

Flower Pot Rim
19 holes x 4 holes
Cut 1

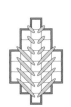

Flower Pot Leaf
5 holes x 8 holes
Cut 2

Flower Pot Stem
3 holes x 22 holes
Cut 1

COLOR KEY		
Yards	**Plastic Canvas Yarn**	
3 (2.8m)	▨ Lavender #05	
1 (1m)	☐ Baby blue #36	
4 (3.7m)	☐ Yellow #57	
	Worsted Weight Yarn	
5 (4.6m)	☐ Soft white	
4 (3.7m)	■ Black	
2 (1.9m)	▨ Camel	
1 (1m)	☐ Pale yellow	
2 (1.9m)	╱ Medium sage green Overcasting	
	╱ Black Straight Stitch	
	Suede Bulky Weight Yarn	
5 (4.6m)	▨ Olive #210-132	
	Chenille Yarn	
6 (5.5m)	■ Garnet #530-113	

Color numbers given are for Uniek Needloft plastic canvas yarn and Lion Brand Yarn Co. Lion Suede bulky weight yarn and Lion Chenille yarn.

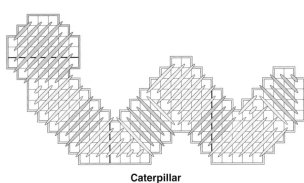

Caterpillar
29 holes x 14 holes
Cut 1

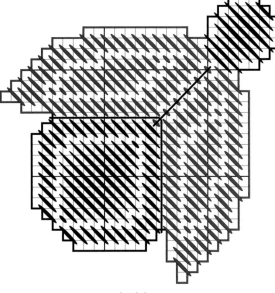

Ladybug
27 holes x 27 holes
Cut 1

Basking Among the Flowers

You'll want to keep this adorable caterpillar in your plants.
Make several of these cute critters for pots around
the house. DESIGN BY PATRICIA KLESH

Skill Level
Beginner

Size
5⅛ inches L x 2⅛ inches H
(13cm x 5.4cm)

Materials
- ¼ sheet 7-count
  plastic canvas
- Worsted weight yarn as
  listed in color key
- 6-strand embroidery floss
  as listed in color key
- #16 tapestry needle
- 9 inches (22.9cm) ⅛-inch-
  wide (3mm) yellow
  satin ribbon
- 1⅜-inch (3.5cm)
  bamboo hat
- ⅛-inch (0.3cm) wood dowel
  in desired length
- Hot-glue gun

Instructions
1. Cut two caterpillars from plastic canvas according to graph.
2. Stitch one caterpillar following graph; reverse remaining caterpillar before stitching.
3. Work black and red floss embroidery when background stitching is completed.
4. Glue dowel to wrong side of one caterpillar (see photo), then

Continued on page 41

Rims & Trims

Jazz up your favorite plants by embellishing their pots with these funky rims and coaster trims. DESIGNS BY MARY T. COSGROVE

Skill Level

Beginner

Size

Pot Rims: ⅝ inches H x 4½ inches in diameter (1.6cm x 11.4cm)

Coaster Trims: ⅝ inches H x 3½ inches in diameter (1.6cm x 8.9cm)

Materials

- ¼ vertical sheet each Uniek QuickCount 7-count plastic canvas in bright pink, bright green, bright blue and bright purple
- 3 (4-inch) Uniek QuickShape plastic canvas radial circles
- Uniek Needloft plastic canvas yarn as listed in color key
- ⅛-inch/3mm-wide satin ribbon as listed in color key
- #16 tapestry needle
- 2½ yards (2.3m) each

- 22-gauge plastic-coated wire: lime green, bright blue and raspberry pink
- Blumenthal Lansing Co. Favorite Findings buttons: 15 purple Ocean Squares #765
  1 pink flower Retro #52
  3 large and 2 small green Bright Flowers #757
  3 large and 2 small pink Bright Flowers #757
  2 large and 3 small yellow Bright Flowers #757
- ¹¹⁄₁₆-inch (1.7cm) purple flower button
- 4 (⁷⁄₁₆-inch/1.1cm) purple flower buttons
- E beads: 40 lime green and 55 bright blue
- 18 yellow seed beads
- Pencil
- Extra thick fast grabbing tacky glue

Cutting & Stitching

1. Cut one rim each and one coaster trim each from bright pink, bright green and bright blue plastic canvas according to graphs (pages 34 and 35), cutting out center hole on bright green pot rim where indicated.

2. From bright purple plastic canvas, cut one 90-hole x 2 hole piece for pot rim center and one 70-hole x 2-hole piece for coaster trim center.

3. Cut three outermost rows of holes from all three plastic canvas radial circles.

Bright Pink

1. For pot rim, twist lime green wire on one end of bright pink canvas to secure, then thread on small purple flower button bring wire up and down through canvas where indicated.

2. For coiled wire, bring wire up where indicated next to flower, wrap wire around pencil several times, then bring wire down at top of canvas where indicated.

3. For beading, bring wire up in next hole, thread on four E beads as indicated (bright blue, lime green, bright blue, lime green), then bring wire down in hole indicated.

4. Continue pattern, coiling wire and adding beads and buttons to end of rim as indicated on graph, placing large purple flower in center.

5. Make a hook at end of pot rim where indicated, by bringing ends of a separate length of wire up through center holes of canvas. Make a 1½-inch (3.8cm) loop, bringing wire back through canvas hole; twist and trim. Twist looped wire and fold over into a hook.

6. Place rim on top of pot and hook wire through adjacent holes on other end of rim to hold in place.

7. For coaster trim, follow steps 2

and 3 for adding coiled wire and beading. **Note:** *No purple flowers will be added to coaster trim.*

8. Using bright pink yarn, Whipstitch short edges of trim together, then Whipstitch bottom edge to one plastic canvas radial circle.

Bright Green

1. For pot rim, work bright pink satin ribbon Cross Stitches across piece, attaching retro pink flower button where indicated while stitching. Glue one yellow seed bead to center of each Cross Stitch.

2. Twist bright blue wire on one end of canvas to secure, then following steps 1 and 2 for bright pink, add coiled wire and purple square buttons across rim where indicated.

3. Make a hook at end of rim with bright blue wire and attach to pot following steps 5 and 6 for bright pink.

4. Work coaster trim following instructions for pot rim.

5. Using fern yarn, Whipstitch short edges of trim together, then Whipstitch bottom edge to one plastic canvas radial circle.

Bright Blue

1. Place bright purple pot rim center in center of bright blue pot rim where indicated with orange lines. Twist raspberry pink wire on one end of canvas to secure, working though both layers.

2. Following steps 1 and 2 for bright pink and working through both layers of canvas, add coiled wire and bright flower buttons across rim where indicated, threading on one bright blue bead in center while attaching each button.

3. Make a hook at end of rim with raspberry pink wire and attach to rim pot, following steps 5 and 6 for bright pink.

4. Place bright purple coaster trim center in center of bright blue coaster trim where indicated with orange lines. Add coiled wire and buttons, working through both layers of canvas following instructions for pot rim.

5. Using bright blue yarn, Whipstitch short edges of trim together, then Whipstitch bottom edge to one plastic canvas radial circle. 🍃

COLOR KEY

Yards	Plastic Canvas Yarn
2 (1.9m)	⁄ Fern #23 Whipstitching
2 (1.9m)	⁄ Bright blue #60 Whipstitching
2 (1.9m)	⁄ Bright pink #62 Whipstitching
	¹⁄₈-inch/3mm-Wide Satin Ribbon
2 (1.9m)	✗ Bright pink Cross Stitch
	⁄ Attach lime green wire
	⁄ Attach bright blue wire
	⁄ Attach raspberry pink wire
	♥ Attach small purple flower button
	♣ Attach large purple flower button
	◆ Attach retro pink flower button
	♡ Attach small pink flower button
	❁ Attach large pink flower button
	♥ Attach small green flower button
	❀ Attach large green flower button
	♡ Attach small yellow flower button
	❁ Attach large yellow flower button
	■ Attach purple square
	○ Attach bright blue E bead
	○ Attach lime green E bead
	○ Attach yellow seed bead

Color numbers given are for Uniek Needloft plastic canvas yarn.

Bright Pink Pot Rim
90 holes x 4 holes
Cut 1 from bright pink

Bright Pink Coaster Trim
70 holes x 4 holes
Cut 1 from bright pink

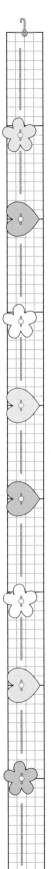

Bright Blue Pot Rim
90 holes x 4 holes
Cut 1 from bright blue

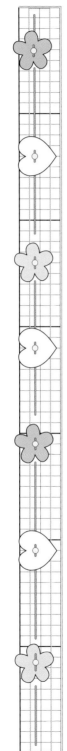

Bright Blue Coaster Trim
70 holes x 4 holes
Cut 1 from bright blue

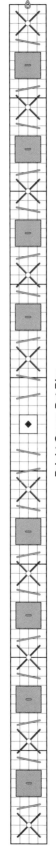

Bright Green Pot Rim
90 holes x 4 holes
Cut 1 from bright green

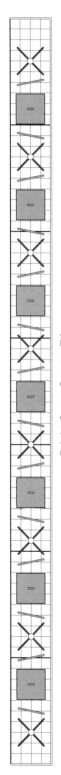

Bright Green Coaster Trim
70 holes x 4 holes
Cut 1 from bright green

Quilt Block Seedling Tray

Plant your tiny seedlings in style this spring by stitching a plastic canvas tray with all the beauty of a country quilt. DESIGN BY ANGIE ARICKX

Skill Level

Beginner

Size

10½ inches W x 13½ inches L x 3½ inches H (26.7cm x 34.3cm x 8.9cm)

Materials

- 2⅓ sheets clear 7-count plastic canvas
- 1 sheet Uniek Quick-Count Christmas green 7-count plastic canvas
- Uniek Needloft plastic canvas yarn as listed in color key
- #16 tapestry needle
- 12 (8-ounce) foam cups

Instructions

1. Cut top from Christmas green plastic canvas; cut sides from clear plastic canvas according to graphs (page 38). Cut one 89-hole x 67-hole piece from clear plastic canvas for tray base.

2. Stitch tray sides following graphs. Tray top and base will remain unstitched.

3. Using holly throughout, Whipstitch long sides to short sides, then Whipstitch sides to base and top.

4. Plant seedlings in foam cups, then insert cups in holes on tray top.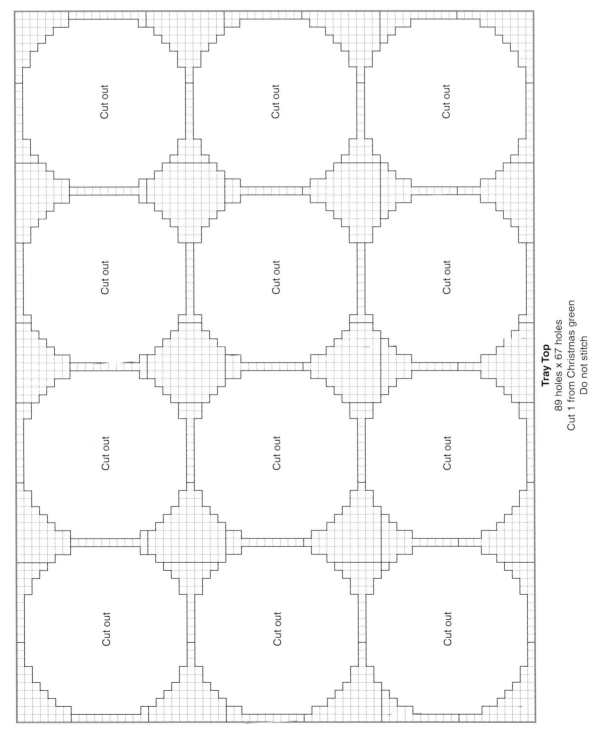

COLOR KEY

Yards	Plastic Canvas Yarn
22 (20.2m)	☐ Fern #23
33 (30.2m)	■ Holly #27
17 (15.6m)	☐ White #41
30 (27.5m)	■ Bright purple #64

Color numbers given are for Uniek Needloft plastic canvas yarn.

Cut out

Tray Top
89 holes x 67 holes
Cut 1 from Christmas green
Do not stitch

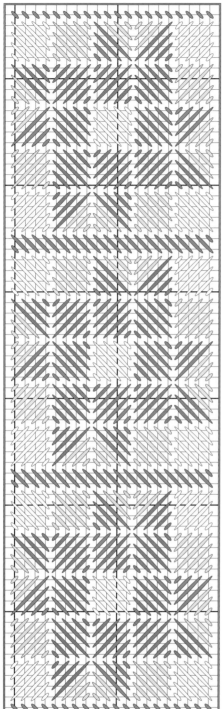

Tray Short Side
67 holes x 21 holes
Cut 2 from clear

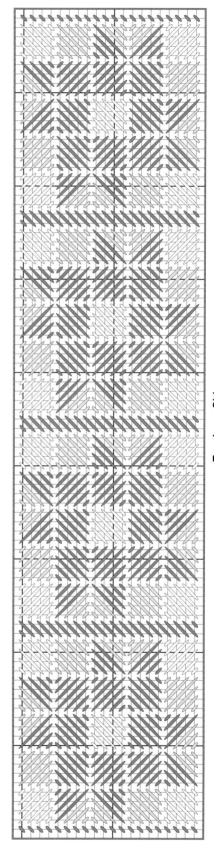

Tray Long Side
89 holes x 21 holes
Cut 2 from clear

COLOR KEY	
Yards	**Plastic Canvas Yarn**
22 (20.2m)	☐ Fern #23
33 (30.2m)	▨ Holly #27
17 (15.6m)	☐ White #41
30 (27.5m)	▨ Bright purple #64

Color numbers given are for Uniek
Needloft plastic canvas yarn.

Whimsical Plant Pokes

Continued from page 19

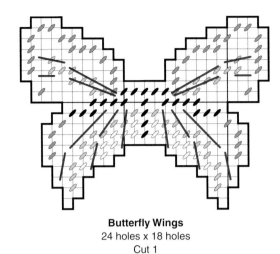

Butterfly Wings
24 holes x 18 holes
Cut 1

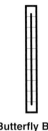

Butterfly Body
1 hole x 10 holes
Cut 1

Continued from page 19

COLOR KEY
BUTTERFLY

Yards	Worsted Weight Yarn
5 (4.6m)	■ Black
2 (1.9m)	■ Purple
2 (1.9m)	■ Medium aqua
1 (1m)	□ Light aqua
4 (3.7m)	Uncoded areas are dark aqua Continental Stitches
	╱ Black Straight Stitch

6-Strand Embroidery Floss

3 (2.8m)	╱ Black Backstitch and Straight Stitch

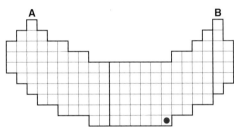

Bird's Nest Front
22 holes x 10 holes
Cut 1

Bird's Nest Large Leaf
5 holes x 7 holes
Cut 3
Stitch 1 as graphed
Stitch 2 with yellow green

Bird's Nest Small Leaf
3 holes x 5 holes
Cut 2
Stitch 1 as graphed
Stitch 2 with clover green

Bird's Nest Egg
4 holes x 5 holes
Cut 3

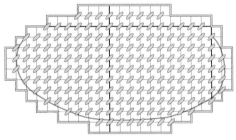

Bird's Nest Back
22 holes x 12 holes
Cut 1

COLOR KEY
BIRD'S NEST

Yards	Worsted Weight Yarn
7 (6.5m)	■ Tan
3 (2.8m)	□ Aqua
3 (2.8m)	□ Yellow green
2 (1.9m)	■ Clover green
1 (1m)	╱ Red brown Straight Stitch and Overcasting

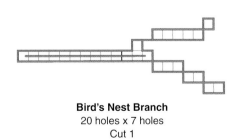

Bird's Nest Branch
20 holes x 7 holes
Cut 1

Butterfly Garden

Use this tiny caddy to hold a plant pot or your favorite candies! DESIGN BY ANGIE ARICKX

Skill Level
Beginner

Size
3¾ inches W x 3¾ inches H x 3¾ inches D (9.5cm x 9.5cm x 9.5cm)

Materials
- 1 sheet 7-count plastic canvas
- Uniek Needloft plastic canvas yarn as listed in color key
- 6-strand embroidery floss as listed in color key
- #16 tapestry needle
- Hot-glue gun

Instructions
1. Cut plastic canvas according to graphs. Cut one 24-hole x 24-hole piece for garden base. Base will remain unstitched.

2. Stitch and Overcast hearts following graph. Stitch remaining pieces, working uncoded background on sides with white Continental Stitches.

3. When background stitching is completed, work embroidery on sides.

4. Following graphs, Whipstitch sides together, then Whipstitch sides to base, Overcast top edges.

5. Using black, Whipstitch wings of each butterfly together where indicated with brackets; Overcast remaining edges.

6. Using photo as a guide, glue assembled butterfly wings to sides, lining them up with stitched heads and antennae. Glue hearts to sides under bows. 🌿

COLOR KEY

Yards	Plastic Canvas Yarn
1 (1m)	Fern #23
3 (2.8m)	Royal #32
12 (11m)	White #41
32 (29.3m)	Camel #43
2 (1.9m)	Purple #46
5 (4.6m)	Watermelon #55
1 (1m)	Yellow #57
4 (3.7m)	Bright blue #60
	Uncoded background on sides is white Continental Stitches
2 (1.9m)	⁄ Black #00 Straight Stitch and Whipstitching
	⁄ Watermelon #55 Backstitch and Straight Stitch
	● Black #00 French Knot
	6-Strand Embroidery Floss
4 (3.7m)	⁄ Black Backstitch and Straight Stitch

Color numbers given are for Uniek Needloft plastic canvas yarn.

Butterfly Garden Side
24 holes x 24 holes
Cut 4

Butterfly Garden Heart
7 holes x 6 holes
Cut 4

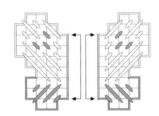

Butterfly Garden Butterfly Wings
5 holes x 9 holes each
Cut 4 sets

Basking Among the Flowers

Continued from page 31

Whipstitch wrong sides of pieces together, working around dowel.
5. Thread ribbon through canvas where indicated and tie in a bow.
6. Glue hat to head. 🍃

COLOR KEY

Yards	Worsted Weight Yarn
9 (8.3m)	Bright green
	6-Strand Embroidery Floss
1 (1m)	⁄ Black
1 (1m)	⁄ Red
	○ Attach yellow ribbon

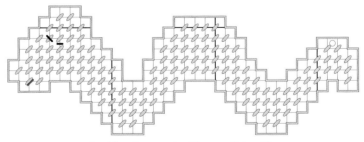

Basking Among the Flowers Caterpillar
34 holes x 12 holes
Cut 2

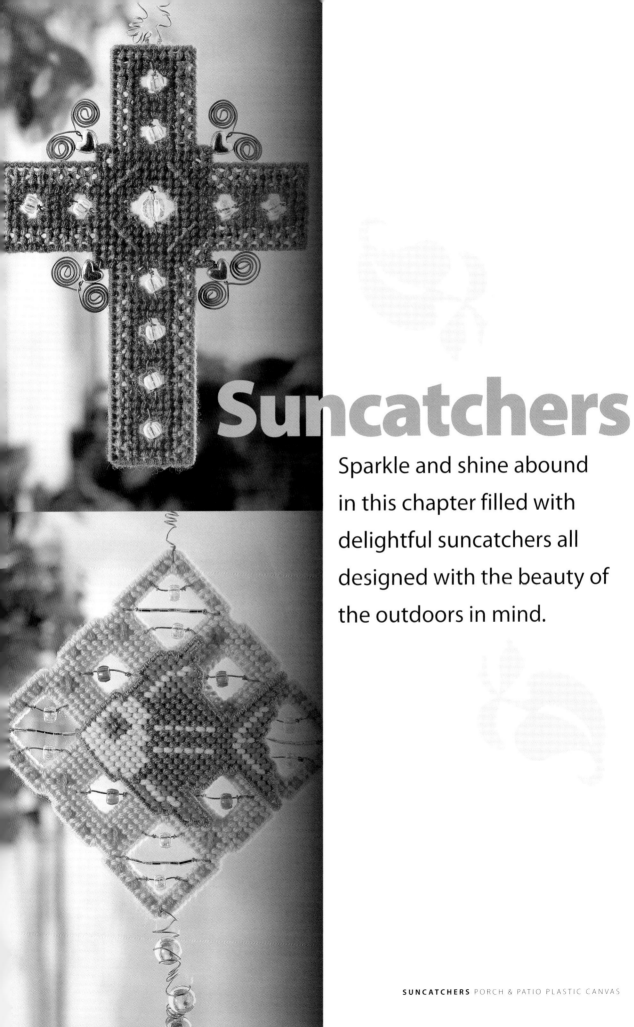

Suncatchers

Sparkle and shine abound in this chapter filled with delightful suncatchers all designed with the beauty of the outdoors in mind.

Floral Suncatchers

Display these bright flowers from hooks or clear cord in a window or among greenery. DESIGNS BY TERRY RICIOLI

Skill Level
Intermediate

Size
Daylily: 6¼ inches W x 6¼ inches H (15.9cm x 15.9cm), excluding hanger

Orchid: 7 inches W x 6½ inches H (17.8cm x 16.5cm), excluding hanger

Sunflower: 4½ inches W x 4½ inches H (11.4cm x 11.4cm), excluding hanger

Materials
Daylily
- ½ sheet 7-count plastic canvas
- Uniek Needloft plastic canvas yarn as listed in color key
- #16 tapestry needle
- Approximately 290 orange transparent 11/0 seed beads
- 3 (3–4mm) orange transparent beads in various shapes.
- 6 x 9mm orange transparent bead in desired shape (sample used rectangle)
- 7mm gold jump ring
- 7 (2-inch-long/5.1cm) gold head pins
- 18 inches (45.7cm) 20-gauge nontarnishing gold wire
- Beading needle
- Yellow and clear thread
- Round-nose pliers
- Wire cutters
- Hot-glue gun

Orchid
- 1 sheet 7-count plastic canvas
- Uniek Needloft plastic canvas yarn as listed in color key
- #16 tapestry needle
- 17 (¼-inch/7mm) gold bugle beads
- 8 x 6mm gold transparent oval bead
- 6mm gold transparent disc or smooth rondelle bead
- 4mm gold transparent round bead
- 17 x 10mm purple transparent teardrop bead
- 7mm gold jump ring
- 2-inch-long (5.1cm) gold head pin
- 18 inches (45.7cm) 20-gauge nontarnishing gold wire
- Beading needle
- Yellow and clear thread
- Round-nose pliers
- Wire cutters
- Hot-glue gun

Sunflower
- ½ sheet 7-count plastic canvas
- Uniek Needloft plastic canvas yarn as listed in color key
- #16 tapestry needle
- 24 (5mm) topaz bicone beads
- 24 inches (61cm) 20-gauge copper or gold wire
- Clear thread
- Wire cutters
- Hot-glue gun

Daylily

1. Cut six petals from plastic canvas according to graph (page 46). Cut wire in six 3-inch (7.6cm) lengths.

2. Holding one length wire behind each petal where indicated with green line, stitch and Overcast petals following graph.

3. To avoid sharp points, use round-nose pliers to bend ends of wires into small loops, trimming any excess wire.

4. Using beading needle and yellow thread, attach four seed beads with one stitch to petals at each place indicated on graph.

5. Thread seed beads on six head pins, leaving ⅜ inch (1cm) free on end. Use needle-nose pliers to turn each end in a small loop. Thread remaining head pin with 6 x 9mm bead, then three 3–4mm beads. Thread on seed beads, leaving ⅜ inch (1cm) free on end. Use needle-nose pliers to turn end of pin in a small loop.

6. Open jump ring and string on loops of head pins. Close ring.

7. Using photo as a guide through step 8, glue three petals together at tips. Glue remaining petals behind and between first three petals. ***Note:*** *Petals will be movable at this point.* Bend petals into desired curves. Glue at additional points as necessary to hold shape.

8. Sew jump ring to center of flower. Gently curve head pins. Head pins may be glued to petals or allowed to hang freely.

9. Attach clear thread hanging loop to tip of one petal.

Orchid

1. Cut one petal A, two petals B and three petals C from plastic canvas according to graphs (page 46). Cut two 3-inch (7.6cm) lengths and three 4-inch (10.2cm) lengths of gold wire.

2. Holding 3-inch (7.6cm) lengths wire behind petals B and 4-inch (10.2cm) lengths behind petals C where indicated with green lines, Continental Stitch and overcast pieces with pink yarn.

3. To avoid sharp points, use round-nose pliers to bend ends of wires into small loops, trimming any excess wire.

4. Stitch petal A following graph, working uncoded areas with pink Continental Stitches. Using pink, Overcast around sides and bottom of petal from dot to dot; Whipstitch remaining two edges together.

5. Using beading needle and yellow thread, attach bugle beads to petal A where indicated on graph.

6. Thread beads on head pin as follows: rondelle, teardrop (wide end first), oval, round. Use round-nose pliers to turn end of pin in a loop.

7. Open jump ring and slip over bars indicated on petal A or sew jump ring in place. Slide loop of head pin on jump ring; close jump ring. **Note:** *Beaded head pin should hang freely.*

8. Using photo as a guide, bend petals in curves as desired. Glue petals B behind petals A, then glue petals C behind petals A and B.

9. Attach clear thread hanging loop to top petal.

Sunflower

1. Cut two base pieces and eight petals from plastic canvas according to graphs. **Note**: *If you want to view suncatcher from both sides, cut*

eight more petals and add another 8 yards of yellow yarn.

2. Stitch and Overcast petals following graphs. Stitch base pieces following graphs. Whipstitch wrong sides of base front and back together with yellow and holly along outside edges and with maple along inside edges.

3. Slide wire under stitches on back and come up through hole indicated at point 1. Wrap wire around bar one time to secure, thread on three beads and bring wire down through hole from front to back at point 2.

4. Slide wire under stitches to point 3, coming out in front. Thread on six beads and bring wire from front to back at point 4.

5. Continue adding beads in this manner, adding eight beads to next three rows, six beads to second last row and three to final row. Finish by wrapping wire around bar one time at point 14 and sliding wire under stitches on back. Trim end.

6. Using photo as a guide, glue petals in groups of two along inside edges between yellow petals on base.

7. Attach clear thread hanging loop to top yellow petal.

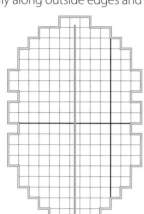

Orchid Petal B
13 holes x 20 holes
Cut 2

COLOR KEY
ORCHID
Yards	Plastic Canvas Yarn
2 (1.9m)	■ Burgundy #03
2 (1.9m)	▨ Tangerine #11
20 (18.3m)	Uncoded areas are pink #07 Continental Stitches
	╱ Pink #07 Overcasting
	╱ Attach bugle bead
	○ Attach jump ring
Color numbers given are for Uniek Needloft plastic canvas yarn.

Daylily Petal
9 holes x 22 holes
Cut 6

COLOR KEY
DAYLILY
Yards	Plastic Canvas Yarn
12 (11m)	▨ Pumpkin #12
5 (4.6m)	□ Yellow #57
	╱ Attach 4 seed beads
Color numbers given are for Uniek Needloft plastic canvas yarn.

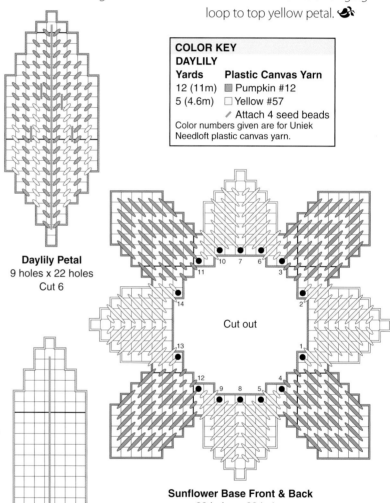

Sunflower Base Front & Back
29 holes x 29 holes
Cut 2

Orchid Petal A
22 holes x 22 holes
Cut 1

Top ↙

Orchid Petal C
7 holes x 27 holes
Cut 3

COLOR KEY
SUNFLOWER
Yards	Plastic Canvas Yarn
10 (9.2m)	▨ Holly #27
18 (16.5m)	□ Yellow #57
1 (1m)	╱ Maple #13 Overcasting
Color numbers given are for Uniek Needloft plastic canvas yarn.

Sunflower Petal
7 holes x 8 holes
Cut 8

Ladybug Duo

This coordinating set will add a delightful touch of whimsy to any room of your home. DESIGN BY ANGIE ARICKX

Skill Level
Intermediate

Size
Suncatcher: 4½ inches W x 4½ inches H (11.4cm x 11.4cm) with legs, excluding hanger

Plant Poke: 2¾ inches W x 2¾ inches H (7cm x 7cm) with legs, excluding poke

Materials
Suncatcher
- ¼ sheet 7-count plastic canvas
- Uniek Needloft plastic canvas yarn listed in color key
- #16 tapestry needle
- 12 inches (30.5cm) black chenille stem
- 10 inches (25.4cm) black thread
- Hot-glue gun

Plant Poke
- ¼ sheet 10-count plastic canvas
- DMC #3 pearl cotton listed in color key
- #18 tapestry needle
- 8 inches (20.3cm) 24-gauge black vinyl coated bead wire
- 9 inches (22.9cm) ¹⁄₁₆ -inch (0.2cm) dowel
- Craft knife
- Hot-glue gun

Instructions

1. Cut plastic canvas according to graph (page 59).

2. Stitch and Overcast pieces following graphs, working uncoded areas on suncatcher ladybug with bittersweet Continental Stitches and uncoded areas on plant poke ladybug with bright orange-red Continental Stitches.

3. For antennae and legs on suncatcher, cut chenille stem in eight equal lengths. Glue lengths to back of suncatcher where indicated at arrows. Bend lengths, using photo as a guide and trimming as desired.

4. Repeat step 3 for plant poke ladybug, using bead wire.

5. For hanger, bring black thread through hole indicated on suncatcher ladybug. Tie ends together in a knot to form a loop for hanging.

6. Sharpen one end of dowel with craft knife. Glue wrong side of plant poke ladybug to other end of dowel (see photo).

Graph on page 59

Greenhouse

Create the illusion of a greenhouse by stitching a house shape and adding green plastic for windows. DESIGN BY GINA WOODS

Skill Level

Intermediate

Size

7⅞ inches W x 5¾ inches H (20cm x 14.6cm), excluding "smoke" and hanger

Materials

- ½ sheet green 7-count plastic canvas
- Worsted weight yarn as listed in color key
- #16 tapestry needle
- 6½ x 4½-inch (16.5 x 11.4cm) green plastic sheet
- Clear iridescent loopy chenille stem
- 9 (7mm) green tinsel pompoms
- 4 (10mm) green tinsel pompoms
- 2 (½-inch/13mm) green tinsel pompoms
- 10 inches (25.4cm) ⅛-inch/ 3mm-wide green satin ribbon
- Hot-glue gun

Project Note

Green plastic sheets may be cut from a plastic envelope or a notebook index divider available at office supply or stationery stores.

Instructions

1. Cut plastic canvas according to graph, cutting out windows on door, house and roof, leaving center horizontal and vertical bars intact. Cut plastic sheet slightly smaller than house and roof portions of greenhouse.

2. Stitch and Overcast following graph, working uncoded areas with medium yellow-green Continental Stitches and using two strands (not graphed) for working stitches on roof. Do not Overcast window edges.

3. When background stitching is completed, use forest green to outline door with Straight Stitches and to work French Knot doorknob. Work green Straight Stitches at shutters and light yellow-green Straight Stitches at windows and at sides of shutters on top windows.

4. Use photo as a guide through step 6. For smoke, cut two 3-inch (7.6cm) lengths chenille stem. Curl as desired and glue behind chimneys.

5. For bushes, glue pompoms as desired to house below bottom windows.

6. Thread ribbon from front to back through holes indicated at roof top. Tie ends together in a bow to make a loop for hanging.

7. Glue green plastic sheet on back side, applying glue sparingly so plastic does not warp.

COLOR KEY	
Yards	Worsted Weight Yarn
20 (18.3m)	☐ Light yellow-green
4 (3.7m)	◼ Green
3 (2.8m)	◻ Medium brown
2 (1.9m)	◼ Dark brown
12 (11m)	Uncoded areas are medium yellow-green Continental Stitches
	⁄ Medium yellow-green Overcasting
	⁄ Light yellow-green Straight Stitch
	⁄ Green Straight Stitch
2 (1.9m)	⁄ Forest green Backstitch
	● Forest green French Knot
	⬤ Attach ribbon hanger

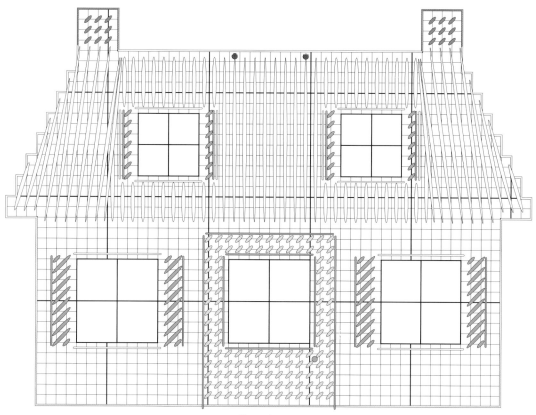

Greenhouse
52 holes x 38 holes
Cut 1

Glimmer Fish

Watch this sweet little fish shimmer when the

sun is out! DESIGN BY MARY T. COSGROVE

Skill Level
Intermediate

Size
7¼ inches W x 7¼ inches H
(18.4cm x 18.4cm), excluding
hanger and wire fringe

Materials
- 1 sheet 7-count
  plastic canvas
- Coats & Clark Red Heart
  Classic worsted weight yarn
  Art. E267 as listed in
  color key
- #16 tapestry needle
- Approximately 3 yards
  (2.8m) 24-gauge light blue
  or clear blue craft wire
- 24 (⅛–¼-inch/5–6mm-
  long) glass light turquoise
  bugle beads
- 4 (6 x 9mm) turquoise
  transparent pony beads
- 8 (6 x 9mm) light pink
  transparent pony beads
- 3 (½-inch/15mm)
  clear marbles
- Pencil

Cutting & Stitching
1. Cut fish and base front and
back from plastic canvas according
to graphs.
2. Stitch and Overcast one fish following graph, working uncoded areas with pink Continental Stitches.
Reverse remaining fish and work all
Continental Stitches in reverse.
3. Stitch base pieces following
graph, working uncoded areas with
mist green Continental Stitches.
Whipstitch wrong sides of base
pieces together along inside and
outside edges with mist green.

Finishing
1. Turn base so Continental
Stitches are horizontal. Beginning
with an 18-inch (45.7cm) length
wire, thread one end through corner of large hole where indicated
with yellow dot. Wrap end tightly
around wire at corner.
2. Thread on six bugle beads,
then bring wire through hole on
opposite corner indicated with
yellow dot. Cut wire, leaving a small
amount to once again wrap end
around wire at corner to secure.
3. In same manner, using
same wire, add one light pink

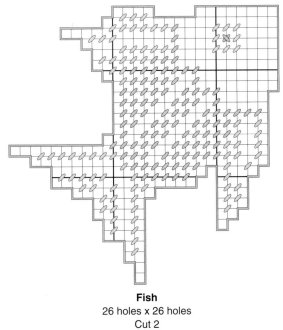

Fish
26 holes x 26 holes
Cut 2
Stitch 1 as graphed
Reverse one and work all
Continental Stitches in reverse

transparent bead above and below bugle beads where indicated with pink dots.

4. Continue adding beads to each large hole, working until 18-inch (45.7cm) length is used up, then begin with another 18-inch (45.7cm) length.

5. In same manner, add turquoise pony beads to small holes where indicated with green dots.

6. Using photo as a guide through step 8, place one fish over center of each side, matching edges on each end. Using medium coral yarn, tack fish pieces together at center of tails and at tips of mouths. *Note: Fish will be joined at corners of large holes.*

7. For hanger, thread one end of a 9-inch (22.9cm) length wire through top hole; twist end around wire to secure. Wrap wire around pencil to coil. Form a loop at top for hanging; twist end to secure.

8. Cut an 18-inch (45.7cm) length of wire. Thread one end through bottom hole; twist end around wire to secure. Wrap wire around three marbles, adding smaller coils between and at bottom of marbles to hold.

COLOR KEY

Yards	Worsted Weight Yarn
6 (6.5m)	▨ Medium coral #252
8 (7.4m)	☐ Parakeet #513
25 (22.9m)	Uncoded areas on base are mist green #681 Continental Stitches
4 (3.7m)	Uncoded areas on fish are pink #737 Continental Stitches
	╱ Mist green #681 Whipstitching

Color numbers given are for Coats & Clark Red Heart Classic worsted weight yarn Art. E267.

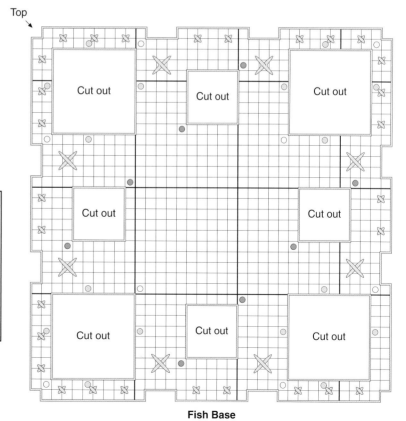

Top

Fish Base
35 holes x 35 holes
Cut 2

Beaded Cross

Enjoy the sparkle and shine of the sunlight when displaying this embellished cross. DESIGN BY MARY T. COSGROVE

Skill Level
Intermediate

Size
5⅞ inches W x 7⅝ inches H (15cm x 19.4cm), excluding hanger

Materials
- 1 sheet 7-count plastic canvas
- Coats & Clark Red Heart Classic worsted weight yarn Art. E267 as listed in color key
- #16 tapestry needle
- 2 yards (1.9m) 24-gauge pink craft wire
- 2 yards (1.9m) 22-gauge blue craft wire
- 4 (12 x 10 mm) silver heart pony beads
- 10 (6 x 9mm) clear transparent pony beads
- 12mm crystal faceted round bead
- Pencil

Cutting & Stitching
1. Cut plastic canvas according to graph, cutting out 11 holes in each cross where indicated.
2. Stitch crosses following graph, working uncoded areas with grenadine Continental Stitches. In center area of crossbar, work longer light periwinkle stitches first, then work shorter stitches over them.
3. With wrong sides facing, Whipstitch inside edges of small cut outs together with grenadine. Whipstitch edges of large cut out together with light periwinkle. Whipstitch outside edges with grenadine.

Wire & Beading
1. To add beads to small cut out areas, begin with an 18-inch (45.7cm) length pink wire. Thread

one end through hole indicated with pink dot. Wrap end tightly around wire at edge.

2. Thread on one clear transparent pony bead, then bring wire through hole indicated with pink dot on opposite side of cut out. Cut wire, leaving a small amount to wrap end around wire at edge to secure.

3. Continue in same manner, adding clear transparent beads to each small cut out, working until 18-inch (45.7cm) length is used up, then begin with another 18-inch (45.7cm) length.

4. Following instructions in step 2, use blue wire to attach 12mm round faceted bead to large center cut out, threading wire through holes indicated with blue dots.

5. Cut four 12-inch (30.5cm) lengths blue wire. Thread one end through each corner indicated with yellow triangle to middle of wire, making ends equal in length. Twist wire at tip of corner.

6. At each corner, thread both ends of wire through silver heart pony bead and twist again. Roll each end in a tight spiral (see photo).

7. For hanger, thread one end of a 12-inch (30.5cm) length pink wire through one top hole where indicated; twist end around wire above edge to secure. Wrap wire around pencil to coil, then thread remaining end through second hole indicated and wrap end around wire above edge to secure. 🐦

Cross
38 holes x 50 holes
Cut 2

COLOR KEY		
Yards	**Worsted Weight Yarn**	
8 (7.4m)	▧ Light periwinkle	
12 (11m)	Uncoded areas are grenadine #730 Continental Stitches	
	╱ Grenadine #730 Whipstitching	
	☆ Attach hanger	
Color numbers given are for Coats & Clark Red Heart Classic worsted weight yarn Art. E267.		

Tulips & Flags

Stitch both of these delightful suncatchers for a floral variation pretty enough to display year-round. DESIGNS BY GINA WOODS

Skill Level

Intermediate

Size

8¼ inches W x 7½ inches H (21cm x 19.1cm), including hanger

Materials

- 1 sheet clear 7-count plastic canvas
- 1 sheet black 7-count plastic canvas
- Worsted weight yarn as listed in color key
- 6-strand embroidery floss as listed in color key
- #16 tapestry needle
- 2 (10-inch/25.4cm) lengths 20-gauge black wire
- Pencil
- 4 (16mm x 12mm) old-world Moroccan antique ivory beads
- Hand-sewing needle
- Camel, black, red and violet thread

Instructions

1. Cut frames, tulips and flags from clear plastic canvas according to graphs. Cut backs from black plastic canvas, carefully cutting out "window panes" (blue areas) on back pieces.

2. Stitch and Overcast pieces following graphs, reversing one small tulip and one small flag before stitching.

3. When background stitching is completed, work medium yellow-green yarn Straight Stitches for stems and for leaves on small flags. Work black floss Backstitches for details on flowers and leaves.

4. Center back pieces behind frames, then sew in place with hand-sewing needle and camel thread.

5. Using photo as a guide, place flowers on bottom sections of back pieces, then sew bottom edges of flowers and blooms to back pieces with matching thread.

6. For hangers, coil center of each wire five times around pencil. Pull wire to loosen coils. Thread one bead on each end, then thread ends through holes indicated on frames. Wrap ends of wire around wire above frames; crimp and push beads down so they rest on tops of frames.

COLOR KEY	
Yards	**Worsted Weight Yarn**
35 (32m)	☐ Camel
35 (32m)	■ Black
15 (13.8m)	▨ Green
10 (9.2m)	☐ Medium yellow-green
6 (5.5m)	☐ Blue violet
5 (4.6m)	■ Red
	⁄ Medium yellow-green Straight Stitch
8 (7.4m)	**6-Strand Embroidery Floss**
	⁄ Black Backstitch
	● Attach wire hanger

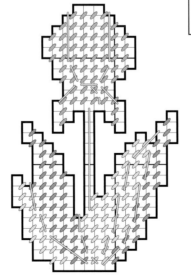

Tulips & Flags Large Flag
16 holes x 25 holes
Cut 1 from clear

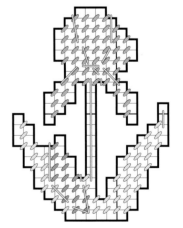

Tulips & Flags Small Flag
15 holes x 20 holes
Cut 2, reverse 1, from clear

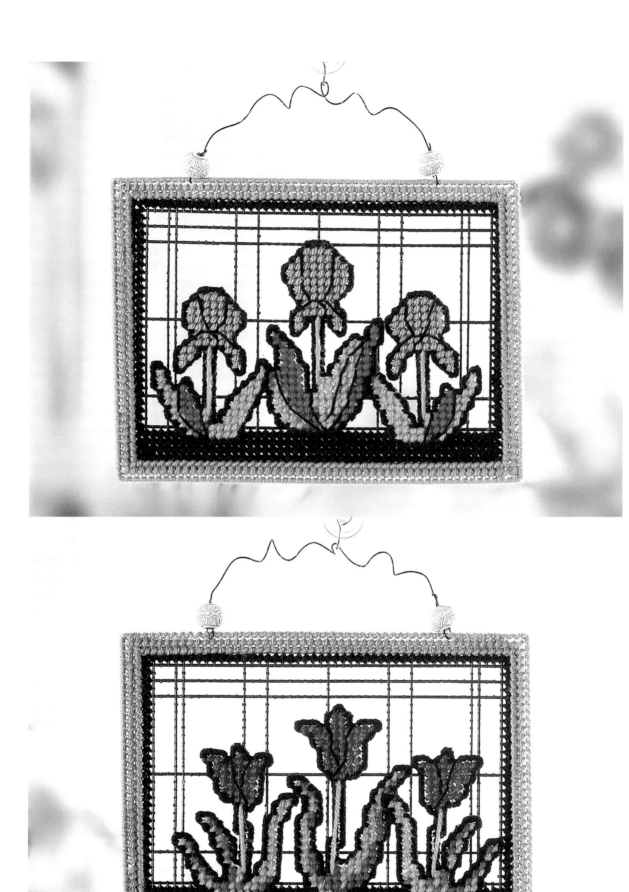

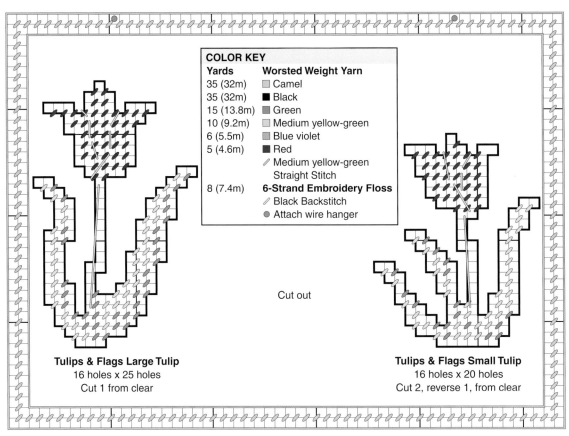

COLOR KEY

Yards	Worsted Weight Yarn
35 (32m)	Camel
35 (32m)	Black
15 (13.8m)	Green
10 (9.2m)	Medium yellow-green
6 (5.5m)	Blue violet
5 (4.6m)	Red
	Medium yellow-green Straight Stitch
8 (7.4m)	**6-Strand Embroidery Floss**
	Black Backstitch
	● Attach wire hanger

Cut out

Tulips & Flags Large Tulip
16 holes x 25 holes
Cut 1 from clear

Tulips & Flags Small Tulip
16 holes x 20 holes
Cut 2, reverse 1, from clear

Tulips & Flags Frame
54 holes x 39 holes
Cut 2 from clear

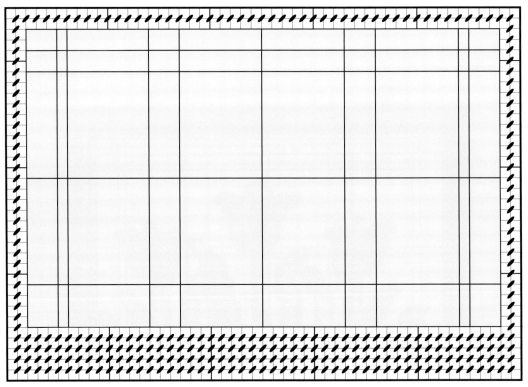

Tulips & Flags Back
50 holes x 35 holes
Cut 2 from black,
cutting away blue areas

Patriotism

Celebrate the good old U.S. of A. with a star-shaped suncatcher embellished with faceted beads.

DESIGN BY LAURA VICTORY

Skill Level
Intermediate

Size
5½ inches W x 7⅞ inches H (14cm x 20cm), including hanger and beads

Materials
- 5-inch Uniek QuickShape plastic canvas star
- Uniek Needloft plastic canvas yarn as listed in color key
- #16 tapestry needle
- 28 (8mm) clear faceted beads
- 8 (8mm) blue faceted beads
- 8 (8mm) red faceted beads
- 5 (4-inch/10.2cm) lengths 26-gauge craft wire
- Hand-sewing needle
- White sewing thread

Instructions
1. Cut gray areas (diamond sections and center section) from plastic canvas star shape according to graph. Do not cut hanging loop off top of star.

2. Stitch and Overcast following graph, repeating pattern in each section of star. Overcast hanging area at top of star, but do not Overcast inside edges adjacent to royal stitching.

3. Thread two clear beads on one length of wire; attach ends where indicated at yellow dots in one diamond cut out. Secure ends in yarn on back side. Repeat with remaining four diamond sections

4. Using hand-sewing needle and white thread, attach remaining beads to each of the four lower tips of star as follows: blue, clear, red, blue, clear, red.

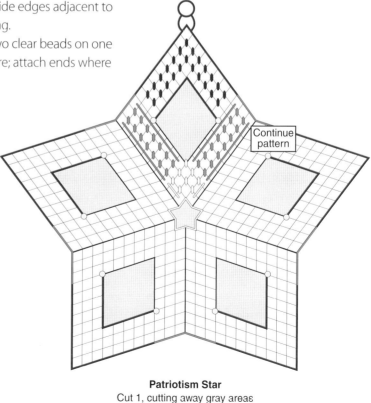

Continue pattern

Patriotism Star
Cut 1, cutting away gray areas

Fanciful Flights

Fluttering in the center of a plastic canvas circle, these dragonflies will dance and frolic in the sunlight. DESIGN BY GINA WOODS

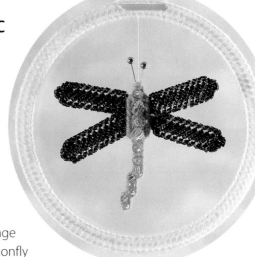

Skill Level

Beginner

Size

Dragonflies: 4 inches W x 3½ inches H (10.2cm x 8.9cm)
Suncatchers: 5¾ inches in diameter (14.6cm), excluding hanger

Materials

- Small amount 7-count plastic canvas
- 6-inch (15.2cm) plastic canvas radial circle
- Worsted weight yarn as listed in color key
- Metallic craft cord as listed in color key
- #16 tapestry needle
- Faceted beads in colors desired:
  5 (4mm); 4 (6mm); 3 (8mm)
- 2 round pearl-headed pins in desired color
- Hand-sewing needle
- Thread to match beads or body color
- 10 inches (25.4cm) ⅛-inch/0.3mm-wide satin ribbon in coordinating color
- Hot-glue gun

Project Notes

Instructions and yardage given are for one dragonfly and one ring.

Both of the samples show coordinating colors of worsted weight yarn used on body and ring and a complementary color of metallic craft cord used on wings.

Beads used were in varying shades of the body color.

Instructions

1. Cut plastic canvas according to graphs, cutting away gray area on ring.

2. Stitch and Overcast pieces following graphs, working ring and body/tail with worsted weight yarn and wings with metallic craft cord.
3. When background stitching is completed, use hand-sewing needle and thread to attach beads to body and tail where indicated on graph.
4. For antennae, push pins into stitching on top back of body.
5. Using photo as a guide through step 6, glue wings to back of body.
6. To hang dragonfly, secure thread to top back of head and to ring where indicated on graph, positioning dragonfly in center of ring.
7. Thread ribbon from front to back through holes indicated at top of ring. Tie ends together in a bow to make a loop for hanging.

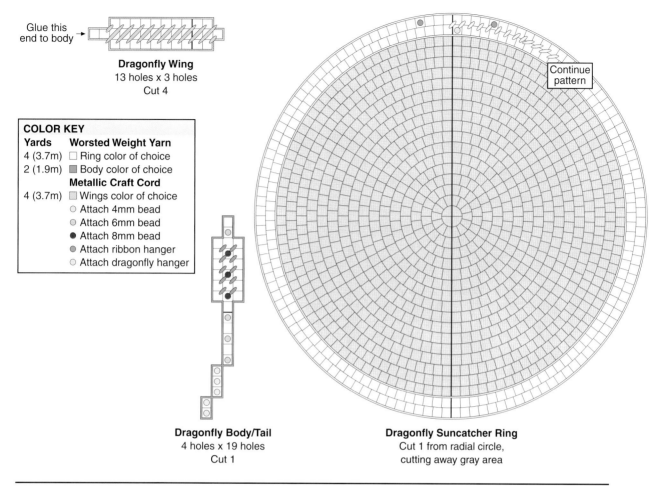

Glue this end to body →

Dragonfly Wing
13 holes x 3 holes
Cut 4

Dragonfly Body/Tail
4 holes x 19 holes
Cut 1

Dragonfly Suncatcher Ring
Cut 1 from radial circle,
cutting away gray area

Continue pattern

Ladybug Duo

Continued from page 47

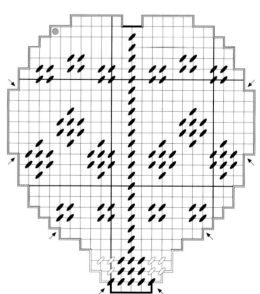

Suncatcher Ladybug
24 holes x 26 holes
Cut 1 from 7-count
Stitch with yarn

Plant Poke Ladybug
24 holes x 26 holes
Cut 1 from 10-count
Stitch with pearl cotton

Tissue Box Covers

Stitch any of these delightful tissue toppers and bring instant sunshine to your day. You'll want to enjoy these anywhere you have plants, whether near a window, outside or on a screened-in porch.

Quilts & Flowers

Switch the look of these pretty toppers with a simple color change. Bright colors give instant modern style, while more muted tones fit well with traditional decor. DESIGNS BY GINA WOODS

Skill Level
Beginner

Size
Fits boutique-style tissue box

Materials
Each
- 1½ sheets 7-count plastic canvas
- Worsted weight yarn as listed in color key
- 6-strand embroidery floss as listed in color key
- #16 tapestry needle

Muted Tones
- Hand-sewing needle
- Eggshell sewing thread

COLOR KEY		
MUTED TONES		
Yards		**Worsted Weight Yarn**
32 (29.3m)	☐	Olive green
23 (21.1m)	☐	Light lavender
7 (6.5m)	◪	Medium lavender
6 (5.5m)	■	Brick red
5 (4.6m)	☐	Terra-cotta
3 (2.8m)	◪	Dark green
60 (54.9m)		Uncoded areas are eggshell Continental Stitches
	⁄	Eggshell Overcasting
	⁄	Dark green Straight Stitch
6-Strand Embroidery Floss		
8 (7.4m)	⁄	Eggshell Straight Stitch

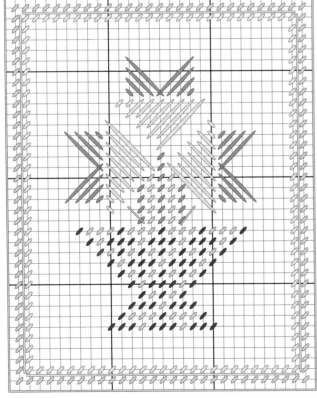

Muted Tones Side
30 holes x 37 holes
Cut 4

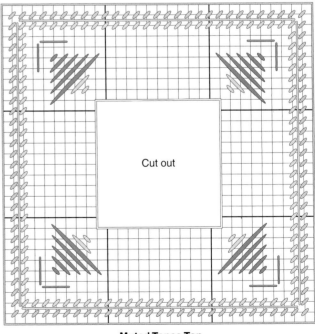

Cut out

Muted Tones Top
30 holes x 30 holes
Cut 1

Instructions

1. Cut plastic canvas according to graphs (pages 62 and 64).

2. Stitch top and sides following graphs, working uncoded areas on bright colors pieces with black yarn Continental Stitches and uncoded areas on muted tones pieces with eggshell yarn Continental Stitches.

3. When background stitching is completed, work lime green Straight Stitches on bright colors pieces and dark green Straight Stitches on muted tones pieces.

4. For bright colors topper, work black floss Backstitches around border of each piece where indicated.

5. Overcast inside edges on top with black yarn. Using dark lavender, Whipstitch sides together, then Whipstitch sides to top; Overcast bottom edges.

6. For muted tones topper, work long eggshell floss Straight Stitches around borders. Using hand-sewing needle and eggshell sewing thread, tack Straight Stitches down in several places.

7. Overcast inside edges on top with eggshell yarn. Using olive green, Whipstitch sides together, then Whipstitch sides to top; Overcast bottom edges. ➴

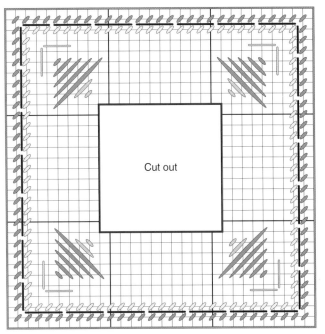

Bright Colors Top
30 holes x 30 holes
Cut 1

Bright Colors Side
30 holes x 37 holes
Cut 4

COLOR KEY		
BRIGHT COLORS		
Yards	**Worsted Weight Yarn**	
32 (29.3m)	■ Periwinkle	
24 (22m)	□ Medium aqua	
7 (6.5m)	▨ Orchid	
6 (5.5m)	▨ Dark aqua	
3 (2.8m)	□ Lime green	
3 (2.8m)	■ Green	
60 (54.9m)	Uncoded areas are black Continental Stitches	
	╱ Black Overcasting	
	╱ Lime green Straight Stitch	
	6-Strand Embroidery Floss	
8 (7.4m)	╱ Black Backstitch	

Flower Boutique

Colored plastic canvas and minimal stitching make this a quick and easy piece that'll add instant flair to your home. DESIGN BY MARY T. COSGROVE

Skill Level
Beginner

Size
Fits boutique-style tissue box

Materials
- 1½ sheets bright purple Uniek QuickCount 7-count plastic canvas
- 1 sheet bright green Uniek QuickCount 7-count plastic canvas
- ⅔ sheet bright pink Uniek QuickCount 7-count plastic canvas
- Uniek Needloft plastic canvas yarn as listed in color key
- #16 tapestry needle
- Embroidery needle
- Blumenthal Lansing Co. Favorite Findings buttons: 4 (½-inch/1.3cm) pink Bright Flowers #757 4 (⅝-inch/1.6cm) pink Bright Flowers #757

Project Note
Use #16 tapestry needle for stitching and Whipstitching; use embroidery needle for attaching buttons.

Instructions

1. Cut one top and four sides from bright purple plastic canvas according to graphs.

2. Following graphs throughout, cut four pink side flowers from bright pink plastic canvas. Cut four stems, four flower centers and one green top flower from bright green plastic canvas.

3. Following instructions for each side through step 5, place one bright green stem where indicated with green highlighted lines; attach by working fern Continental Stitches on stem and Backstitches for veins on leaves.

4. Place one bright pink flower where indicated with deep pink highlighted lines and one bright green flower center in middle of pink flower, indicated with green highlighted lines. Using fern, Whipstitch together through all three layers around edges of flower center.

5. Using embroidery needle and fern yarn, attach one ½-inch (1.3cm) pink flower button to center of flower where indicated.

6. Place green top flower on top per top along green highlighted lines, then Whipstitch together along inside edges with fern.

7. Using embroidery needle and fern yarn, attach ⅝-inch (1.6cm) pink flower button to each flower petal where indicated.

8. Using bright purple yarn, Whipstitch sides together, then Whipstitch sides to top. Bottom edges will remain unstitched. ⟾

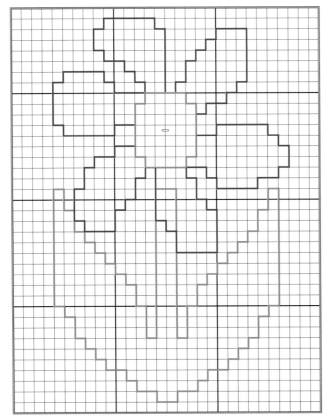

Flower Boutique Side
30 holes x 38 holes
Cut 4 from bright purple

Flower Center
6 holes x 7 holes
Cut 4 from bright green
Do not stitch

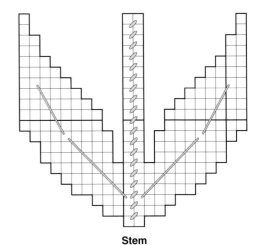

Stem
22 holes x 20 holes
Cut 4 from bright green

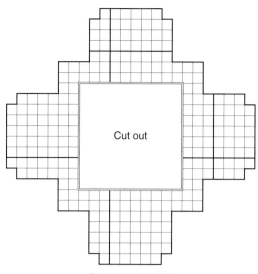

Green Top Flower
24 holes x 24 holes
Cut 1 from bright green
Do not stitch

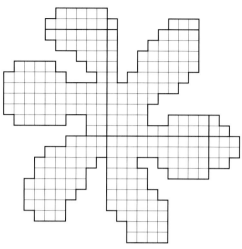

Pink Side Flower
23 holes x 22 holes
Cut 4 from bright pink
Do not stitch

COLOR KEY

Yards	Plastic Canvas Yarn
6 (5.5m)	☐ Fern #23
4 (3.7m)	✎ Bright purple #64 Whipstitching
	✎ Fern #23 Backstitch
	⚊ Attach ½-inch (1.3cm) button
	▬ Attach ⅝-inch (1.6cm) button

Color numbers given are for Uniek Needloft plastic canvas yarn.

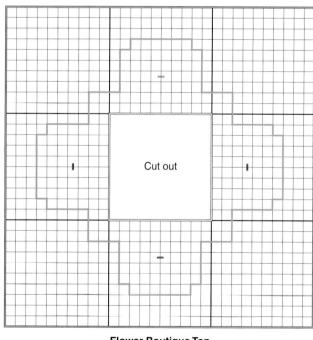

Flower Boutique Top
30 holes x 30 holes
Cut 1 from bright purple
Do not stitch

Garden Collage

Pretty shades of green combine on this striking tissue topper that features everything garden! DESIGN BY GINA WOODS

Skill Level

Beginner

Size

Fits boutique-style tissue box

Materials

- 1½ sheets 7-count plastic canvas
- Worsted weight yarn as listed in color key
- 6-strand embroidery floss as listed in color key
- #16 tapestry needle

Instructions

1. Cut plastic canvas according to graphs.

2. Stitch pieces following graphs, working uncoded areas on white background with lime green Continental Stitches and uncoded areas on yellow background with pale green Continental Stitches.

3. When background stitching is completed, using 4 plies yarn through step 4, work lime green Backstitches and Straight Stitches on borders and on planter block. Work bronze Straight Stitches for roofs on birdhouses.

4. Work black French Knots for head on ladybugs and bronze French Knots for flowers in pumpkin planters.

5. Use 2 plies bronze to work French Knots on holly green borders.

6. Using black embroidery floss, work Straight Stitches and French Knots on ladybugs.

7. Overcast inside edges on top with lime green yarn. Using aqua, Whipstitch sides together, then Whipstitch sides to top; Overcast bottom edges.

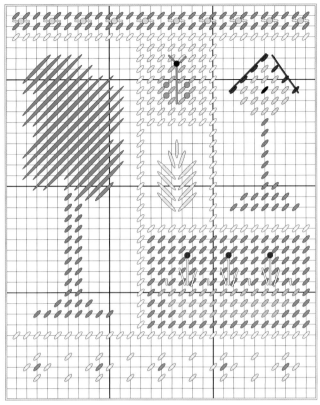

Garden Collage Side
30 holes x 37 holes
Cut 4

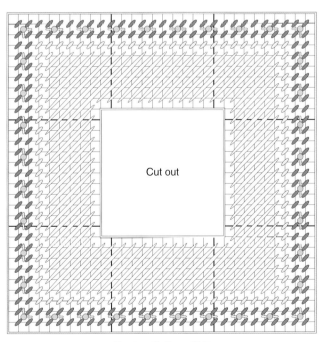

Garden Collage Side
30 holes x 30 holes
Cut 1

Springtime Birdhouse

Add tiny embellishments to this fancy birdhouse for a little extra dimension. Pretty flowers and trellis work would make any bird happy! DESIGN BY ANGIE ARICKX

Skill Level

Intermediate

Size

Fits boutique-style tissue box

Materials

- 2½ sheets 7-count plastic canvas
- Coats & Clark Red Heart Super Saver worsted weight yarn Art. E300 as listed in color key
- Uniek Needloft plastic canvas yarn as listed in color key
- Uniek Needloft metallic craft cord as listed in color key
- #16 tapestry needle
- 2 (1¼-inch/3.2cm) mushroom birds
- 2 (1¾-inch/4.4cm-long) miniature garden benches
- 2 yards (1.9m) decorative green ribbon with (½-inch/1.3cm) dark pink yo-yo flowers *or* 2 yards (1.9m) green ribbon and 34 (½-inch/1.3cm) dark pink flowers
- 1 inch (2.5cm) ³⁄₁₆-inch (0.5cm) dowel, painted white
- Thumbtack
- Hot-glue gun

Project Note

Sample used miniature garden benches with flowers and watering can on seat.

Instructions

1. Cut plastic canvas according to graphs (pages 72 and 73).

2. Following graphs throughout, stitch and Overcast doors and trellises. Stitch remaining pieces. Work gold metallic craft cord French Knots on doors when background stitching and Overcasting are completed.

3. Overcast inside edges of front with soft white. Using warm brown, Whipstitch front and back to sides; Overcast top and bottom edges.

4. Using Windsor blue, Overcast bottom edges of roof pieces and eaves from dot to dot. Whipstitch top edges of roof pieces together, then Whipstitch side edges of assembled roof to top edges of eaves.

5. Insert thumbtack from back to front on front piece where indicated with green dot. Firmly impale white dowel onto thumbtack.

6. Following graphs, weave decorative ribbon through trellis, placing flowers attached to ribbon where indicated or glue flowers in place if using flowers not attached to ribbon; tack ends of ribbon in place with glue.

7. Using photo as a guide throughout, glue roof to birdhouse. Making sure bottom edges are even, center and glue large trellises to sides and small trellises to front and back. Glue benches to sides and doors to front. Glue one bird on perch and one on peak of roof.

8. Insert tissue box sideways in bottom of birdhouse so tissue comes out bottom opening on front.

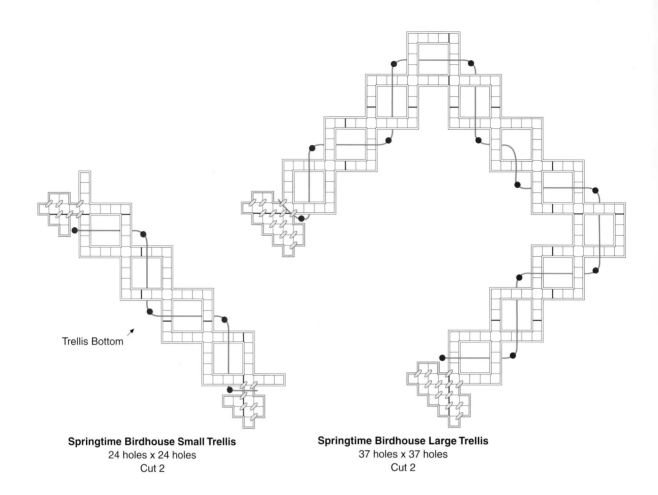

Trellis Bottom

Springtime Birdhouse Small Trellis
24 holes x 24 holes
Cut 2

Springtime Birdhouse Large Trellis
37 holes x 37 holes
Cut 2

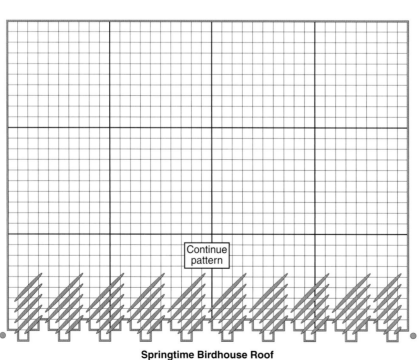

Continue
pattern

Springtime Birdhouse Roof
39 holes x 30 holes
Cut 2

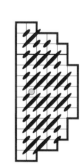

Springtime Birdhouse Large Door
6 holes x 13 holes
Cut 2

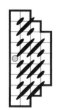

Springtime Birdhouse Small Door
4 holes x 9 holes
Cut 2

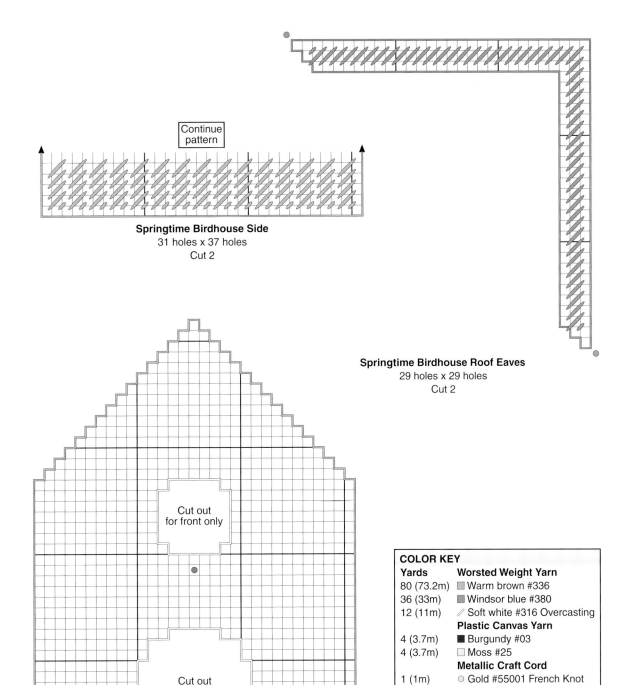

Springtime Birdhouse Side
31 holes x 37 holes
Cut 2

Continue pattern

Springtime Birdhouse Roof Eaves
29 holes x 29 holes
Cut 2

Cut out for front only

Cut out for front only

Continue pattern

Spring Birdhouse Front & Back
31 holes x 52 holes
Cut 2

COLOR KEY

Yards	Worsted Weight Yarn
80 (73.2m)	Warm brown #336
36 (33m)	Windsor blue #380
12 (11m)	Soft white #316 Overcasting
	Plastic Canvas Yarn
4 (3.7m)	Burgundy #03
4 (3.7m)	Moss #25
	Metallic Craft Cord
1 (1m)	Gold #55001 French Knot
	Flower placement
	Insert thumbtack

Color numbers given are for Coats & Clark Red Heart Super Saver worsted weight yarn Art. E300 and Uniek Needloft plastic canvas yarn and metallic craft cord.

Hot-Air Balloon Topper

Drift away on fluffy clouds and a warm breeze with this brightly colored tissue topper featuring a hot-air balloon. DESIGN BY NANCY DORMAN

Skill Level
Beginner

Size
Fits boutique-style tissue box

Materials
- 1 sheet 7-count plastic canvas
- Worsted weight yarn as listed in color key
- #16 tapestry needle

Project Note
Depending on size of boutique-style tissue box, this topper may be a very tight fit.

Instructions
1. Cut one top and four sides from plastic canvas according to graphs.
2. Following graphs and using double strand throughout all stitching, work all white Smyrna Cross Stitch borders first.
3. Stitch hot-air balloons next, then stitch tops of trees with green and blue sky background with light blue. Work light blue stitches on

top. Using 1 strand tan, Straight Stitch ropes when all background stitching is completed.

4. Using white Binding Stitch or regular Overcast Stitch/Whipstitch throughout, Whipstitch sides together, then Whipstitch sides to top. Overcast inside edges of top and bottom edges of sides.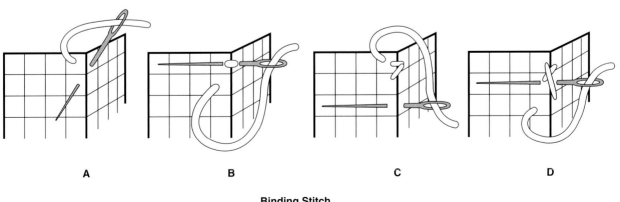

COLOR KEY	
Yards	**Worsted Weight Yarn**
60 (54.9m)	☐ White (2 strands)
50 (45.7m)	☐ Light blue (2 strands)
10 (9.2m)	■ Green (2 strands)
10 (9.2m)	▨ Medium rose pink (2 strands)
8 (7.4m)	■ Medium blue (2 strands)
8 (7.4m)	☐ Light yellow (2 strands)
1 (1m)	▨ Tan (2 strands)
	⁄ Tan Straight Stitch (1 strand)

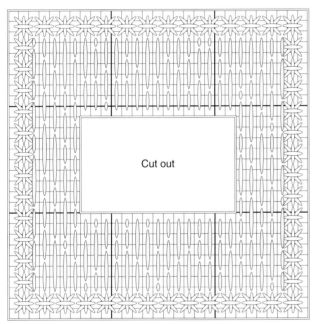

Hot-Air Balloon Top
29 holes x 29 holes
Cut 1

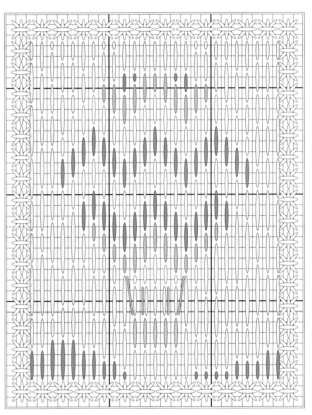

Hot-Air Balloon Side
29 holes x 37 holes
Cut 4

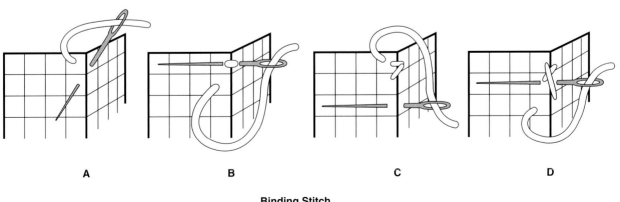

A   B   C   D

Binding Stitch

He Loves Me ...
He Loves Me Not

Pick daisies to your heart's content! This coordinating topper and picnic pocket are overflowing with blooms. DESIGNS BY ALIDA MACOR

Skill Level

Beginner

Size

Tissue Topper: Fits boutique-style tissue box
Picnic Pocket: 4¾ inches W x 9¾ inches H (12.1cm x 24.8cm)

Materials

- 1½ sheets clear 7-count plastic canvas
- 1 sheet blue 7-count plastic canvas
- ¾ sheet white 7-count plastic canvas
- Worsted weight yarn as listed in color key
- #16 tapestry needle
- Hand-sewing needle
- Light orange sewing thread

COLOR KEY

Yards	Worsted Weight Yarn
57 (52.2m)	▨ Blue
13 (11.9m)	☐ White
11 (10.1m)	▨ Chartreuse
10 (9.2m)	▨ Medium brown
6 (5.5m)	▨ Rose
3 (2.8m)	▨ Light orange
	╱ Chartreuse Backstitch and Straight Stitch
	○ Attach daisy

Instructions

1. For topper, cut four sides and one top from clear plastic canvas; cut 12 daisies from white plastic canvas according to graphs (this page and page 79).

2. For pocket, cut one front and one back from blue plastic canvas (pages 78 and 79); cut three daisies from white plastic canvas (page 79).
3. Stitch 12 daisies, topper sides and top following graphs,

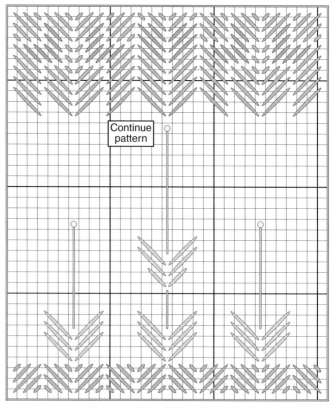

He Loves Me ... He Loves Me Not
Topper Side
31 holes x 37 holes
Cut 4 from clear

working chartreuse Straight
Stitches on sides when background
stitching is completed.

4. Overcast inside edges of top and
bottom edges of sides. Daisy edges
are not Overcast.

5. Using hand-sewing needle and
light orange thread, tack three daisies to each side where indicated
on graph.

6. Whipstitch sides together, then
Whipstitch sides to top.

7. Stitch pocket front and three
daisies following graphs, leaving
light orange Smyrna Cross Stitches
on daisies unworked at this time.
Pocket back will remain unstitched.

8. Overcast top edges of front
from blue dot to blue dot. Do
not Overcast daisies. Place daisies
where indicated on front and attach each with light orange Smyrna
Cross Stitch.

9. Place front on back; Whipstitch
together around side and
bottom edges from blue dot to
blue dot. ⌒

COLOR KEY

Yards	Worsted Weight Yarn
57 (52.2m)	▨ Blue
13 (11.9m)	☐ White
11 (10.1m)	▨ Chartreuse
10 (9.2m)	▨ Medium brown
6 (5.5m)	▨ Rose
3 (2.8m)	☐ Light orange
	╱ Chartreuse Backstitch and Straight Stitch
	○ Attach daisy

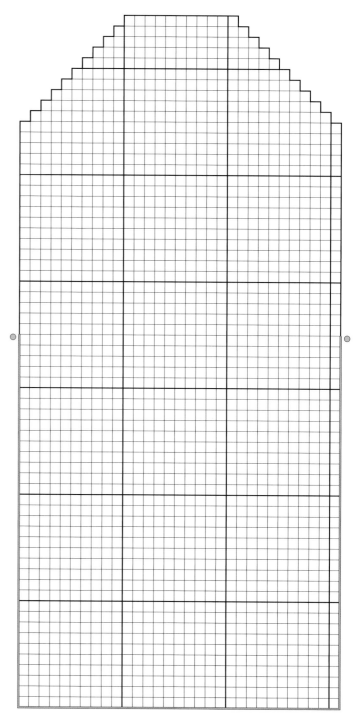

He Loves Me ... He Loves Me Not
Picnic Pocket Back
31 holes x 65 holes
Cut 1 from blue
Do not stitch

**He Loves Me ... He Loves Me Not
Daisy**
11 holes x 11 holes
Cut 12 from white for topper
Cut 3 from white for pocket

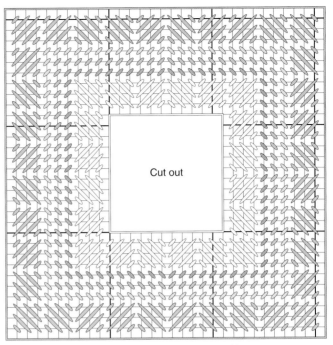

Cut out

**He Loves Me ... He Loves Me Not
Topper Top**
31 holes x 31 holes
Cut 1 from clear

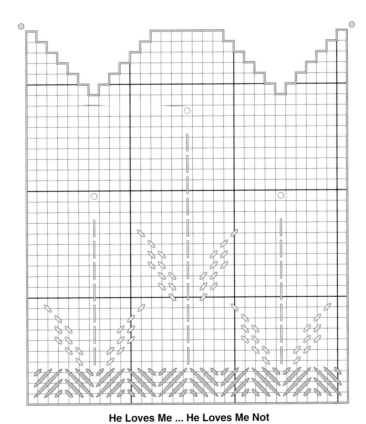

**He Loves Me ... He Loves Me Not
Picnic Pocket Front**
31 holes x 35 holes
Cut 1 from blue

Summer Basket

Brighten your home even on a cloudy day with a tissue topper adorned with baskets brimming with summer flowers. DESIGN BY TERRY RICIOLI

Skill Level
Beginner

Size
Fits boutique-style tissue box

Materials
- 2½ sheets 7-count plastic canvas
- Uniek Needloft plastic canvas yarn as listed in color key
- #16 tapestry needle
- Hot-glue gun

Instructions
1. Cut plastic canvas according to graphs.

2. Stitch top and sides following graphs. Overcast inside edges of top and bottom edges of sides.

3. Stitch and Overcast five flowers with pink as graphed and five each replacing pink with lemon and baby blue.

4. Stitch and Overcast five flower centers with watermelon as graphed and five each replacing watermelon with yellow and bright blue.

5. Stitch and Overcast baskets and leaves following graphs.

6. Using eggshell, Whipstitch sides together, then Whipstitch sides to top.

7. Making sure bottom edges are even, center and glue one basket to each side under stem.

8. Using photo as a guide through step 9, glue yellow flower centers to lemon flowers, watermelon flower centers to pink flowers and bright blue flower centers to baby blue flowers.

9. Glue flowers and leaves to sides and top. ⌒

Summer Basket Flower Center
4 holes x 4 holes
Cut 15
Stitch 5 as graphed
Stitch 5 each, replacing
watermelon with yellow
and bright blue

COLOR KEY

Yards	Plastic Canvas Yarn
14 (12.9m)	☐ Pink #07
12 (11m)	☐ Lemon #20
16 (14.7m)	☐ Moss #25
12 (11m)	☐ Baby blue #36
75 (68.6m)	☐ Eggshell #39
10 (9.2m)	▨ Watermelon #55
8 (7.4m)	☐ Yellow #57
8 (7.4m)	▨ Bright blue #60

Color numbers given are for Uniek
Needloft plastic canvas yarn.

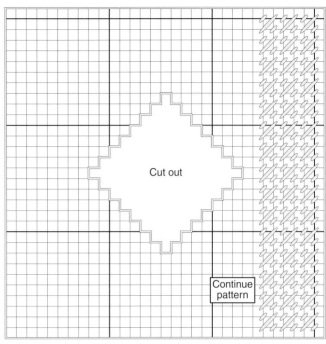

Summer Basket Top
31 holes x 31 holes
Cut 1

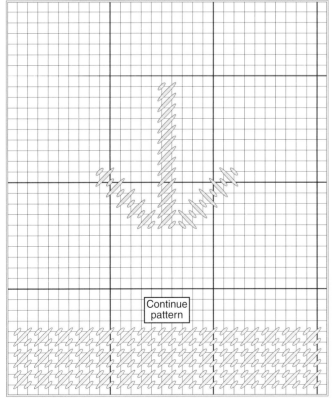

Summer Basket Side
31 holes x 37 holes
Cut 4

Summer Basket Leaves
7 holes x 5 holes
Cut 15

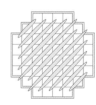

Summer Basket Flower
8 holes x 8 holes
Cut 15
Stitch 5 as graphed
Stitch 5 each, replacing
pink with lemon
and baby blue

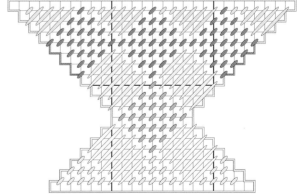

Summer Basket
28 holes x 18 holes
Cut 4

Welcome Signs & Door Decor

Delight friends and family alike with whimsical decor stitched just for your porch and patio. From friendly birds to fancy floral motifs, you'll find something in this chapter to fit your fancy!

Welcome to Our Nest

Not straying too far from the nest, these three baby birds will welcome all your guests and bring a smile to their faces! DESIGN BY DEBORAH SCHEBLEIN

Skill Level

Beginner

Size

Approximately 10⅛ inches W x 17⅛ inches H (25.7cm x 43.5cm), including flying baby birds

Materials

- 1 sheet 7-count plastic canvas
- Worsted weight yarn as listed in color key
- #16 tapestry needle
- 8 (7mm) movable eyes
- 2 yards (1.9m) black cloth-covered wire
- 1 yard (1m) ⅛-inch/ 3mm-wide white satin ribbon
- Hot-glue gun

Instructions

1. Cut plastic canvas according to graphs (this page and page 86), carefully cutting baby bird B apart at red lines.
2. Overcast beaks with yellow. Stitch and Overcast remaining pieces following graphs, working uncoded areas on sign with medium brown Continental Stitches.

3. Work blue Straight Stitches on baby bird B when background stitching is completed. Glue beaks and eyes to baby bird A, baby bird C and both birds in nest.
4. Cut wire in six 6-inch (15.2cm) lengths. Form each length into foot and leg, using pattern (page 86) as a guide.
5. Insert legs from front to back through holes indicated on graphs. Pull legs through until desired length on front (see photo). Glue legs to wrong sides of bodies to secure.
6. Cut three varying lengths of ribbon. Glue one end of each ribbon to back of nest where indicated with arrows. Center and glue remaining ends to top center back side of each baby bird. 🦅

COLOR KEY	
Yards	**Worsted Weight Yarn**
14 (12.9m)	▨ Green
8 (7.4m)	▨ Gold
6 (5.5m)	▨ Blue
4 (3.7m)	▢ White
2 (1.9m)	▢ Peach
14 (12.9m)	Uncoded area is medium brown Continental Stitches
	╱ Medium brown Overcasting
1 (1m)	╱ Yellow Overcasting
	╱ Blue Straight Stitch
	● Attach movable eye
	♡ Attach beak
	● Attach leg

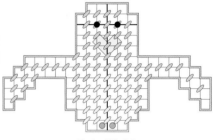

Baby Bird A
20 holes x 12 holes
Cut 1

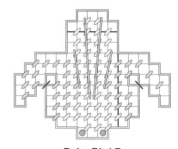

Baby Bird B
15 holes x 12 holes
Cut 1

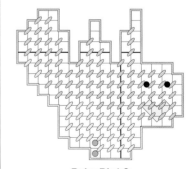

Baby Bird C
16 holes x 14 holes
Cut 1

COLOR KEY

Yards	Worsted Weight Yarn
14 (12.9m)	▨ Green
8 (7.4m)	▨ Gold
6 (5.5m)	☐ Blue
4 (3.7m)	☐ White
2 (1.9m)	☐ Peach
14 (12.9m)	Uncoded area is medium brown Continental Stitches
	⁄ Medium brown Overcasting
1 (1m)	⁄ Yellow Overcasting
	⁄ Blue Straight Stitch
	● Attach movable eye
	♡ Attach beak
	⬤ Attach leg

Welcome to Our Nest Beak
2 holes x 2 holes
Cut 4

Foot & Leg
Make 6 each from 6 inches
(15.2cm) black cloth-covered wire

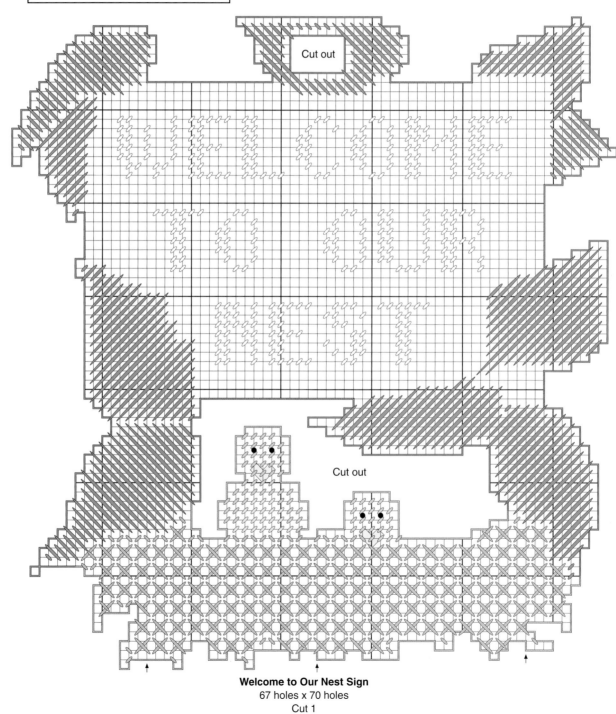

Welcome to Our Nest Sign
67 holes x 70 holes
Cut 1

Birdhouse Welcome

Use a variety of yarns to add texture to this country welcome that's for more than just birds. DESIGN BY PAM BULL

Skill Level
Intermediate

Size
Birdhouse Welcome: 15¼ inches W x 11 inches H x 1¼ inches D (38.7cm x 27.9cm x 3.2cm), excluding hanging heart
Hanging Heart: 2⅝ inches W x 2⅞ inches H (6.7cm x 7.3cm), excluding hanger and bow

Materials
- 1 artist-sized sheet 7-count plastic canvas
- Worsted weight yarn as listed in color key
- Lion Brand Yarn Lion Suede Article #210 bulky weight yarn as listed in color key
- Lion Brand Yarn Homespun Article #790 bulky weight yarn as listed in color key
- #16 tapestry needle
- ½ inch (1.3cm) round pewter button
- ¾ inch (1.9cm) round pewter button
- 2¼ yards (2.1m) twine
- Hot-glue gun

Cutting & Stitching
1. Cut plastic canvas according to graphs (pages 89, 90 and 91). Cut two 4-hole x 2-hole pieces for lower birdhouse top.
2. Continental Stitch lower birdhouse top pieces with shaker yarn. Stitch and Overcast heart, upper birdhouse roof front, lower birdhouse roof and peg front pieces following graphs.
3. Stitch remaining pieces following graphs. Work off-white, heather gray, medium sage and shaker Backstitches and Straight Stitches when background stitching is completed.
4. Overcast peg board around side and bottom edges, leaving top edge unstitched.
5. Using shaker yarn throughout and following assembly diagram (page 90) through step 6, Whipstitch lower birdhouse sides to lower birdhouse. Whipstitch one 2-hole edge of lower birdhouse top pieces to lower birdhouse between brackets, then Whipstitch top pieces to side pieces.
6. Using off-white, Whipstitch upper birdhouse sides to upper birdhouse and to lower birdhouse top pieces. Using heather gray, Whipstitch top edges of upper roof sides together, then Whipstitch roof sides to upper birdhouse front and sides. Overcast all remaining edges of assembled birdhouse.
7. Using off-white, Whipstitch sign top to sign sides, then Whipstitch top and sides to front.
8. With wrong side of shelf lip facing right side of shelf back, Whipstitch back edge of lip to top edge of back.
9. For each peg, Whipstitch short edges of one peg side together, forming a tube; Overcast remaining edges.

Final Assembly
1. Using medium sage yarn, attach ½ inch (1.3cm) button to upper birdhouse where indicated on graph, tying a knot in front. Repeat with ¾ inch (1.9cm) button, attaching to lower birdhouse front where indicated.
2. Glue bottom edges of assembled birdhouse near back edge of shelf lip, placing birdhouse about 6 holes from right edge. Repeat for sign, placing it about three holes from left edge.
3. Using photo as a guide, glue upper birdhouse front and lower birdhouse roof in place.
4. Center shelf over peg board, making top edges even; glue in place.

5. Cut one 8-inch (20.3cm) length twine. Tie in a single bow and glue to front of heart where indicated on graph. Trim ends as desired.

6. Cut one 10-inch (25.4cm) length twine. Tie ends together in a knot forming a loop for hanging. Glue knot to center back of heart.

7. Cut remaining length of twine in half. Put lengths together and tie in a knot about 7½–8 inches (19.2–20.3cm) from right end. Using photo as a guide, glue bow to shelf lip in front of bottom left corner of birdhouse. Glue tails to shelf lip and shelf back as desired, trimming ends as needed.

8. Center and glue one peg front over end of one peg side. Repeat with remaining pegs. Placing seam at bottom, glue backs of pegs to peg board where indicated with blue lines. Hang heart on one peg.

9. Hang assembled welcome as desired.

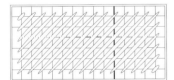

Birdhouse Welcome Peg Side
7 holes x 15 holes
Cut 3

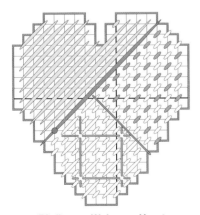

Birdhouse Welcome Heart
17 holes x 18 holes
Cut 1

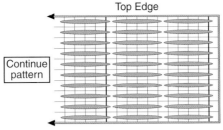

Top Edge

Continue pattern

Birdhouse Welcome Shelf Back
111 holes x 10 holes
Cut 1

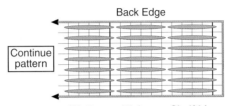

Back Edge

Continue pattern

Birdhouse Welcome Shelf Lip
111 holes x 7 holes
Cut 1

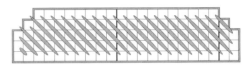

Lower Birdhouse Roof
22 holes x 5 holes
Cut 1

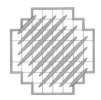

Birdhouse Welcome Peg Front
8 holes x 8 holes
Cut 3

COLOR KEY		
Yards	**Worsted Weight Yarn**	
51 (46.7m)	☐ Off-white	
8 (7.4m)	▨ Heather gray	
3 (2.8m)	▦ Medium sage	
	╱ Off-white Straight Stitch	
	╱ Heather gray Backstitch and Straight Stitch	
	╱ Medium sage Straight Stitch	
	Bulky Weight Yarn	
24 (22m)	▨ Mocha #210-125	
6 (5.5m)	☐ Shaker #301	
	╱ Shaker #301 Backstitch	
	● Attach ½-inch (1.3cm) button	
	● Attach ¾-inch (1.9cm) button	
	● Attach twine bow	

Color numbers given are for Lion Brand Yarn Lion Suede bulky weight yarn Article #210 and Homespun bulky weight yarn Article #790.

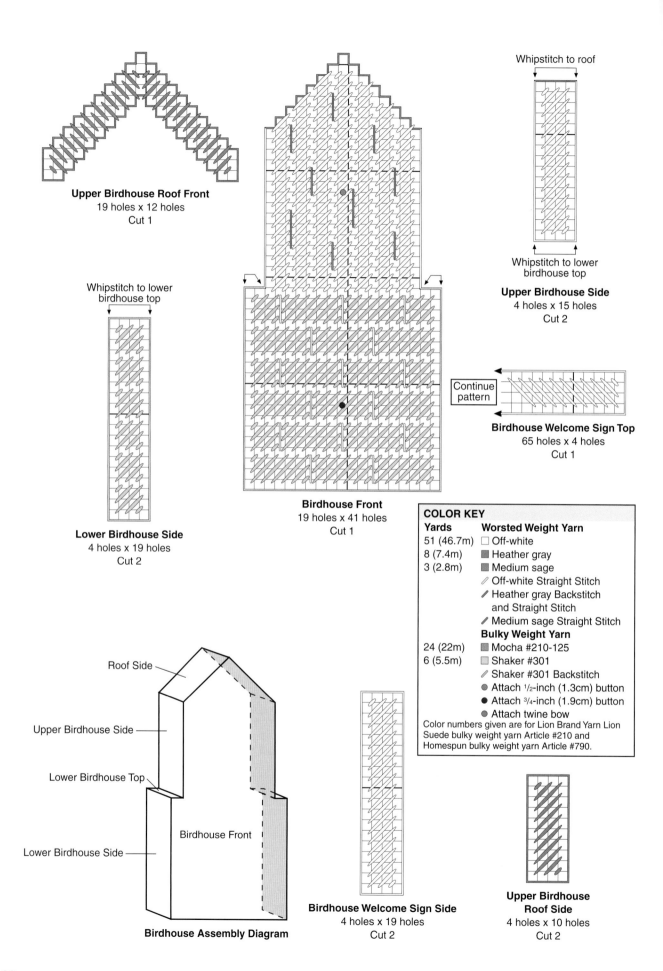

Upper Birdhouse Roof Front
19 holes x 12 holes
Cut 1

Whipstitch to roof

Upper Birdhouse Side
4 holes x 15 holes
Cut 2

Whipstitch to lower
birdhouse top

Whipstitch to lower
birdhouse top

Lower Birdhouse Side
4 holes x 19 holes
Cut 2

Birdhouse Front
19 holes x 41 holes
Cut 1

Continue
pattern

Birdhouse Welcome Sign Top
65 holes x 4 holes
Cut 1

COLOR KEY

Yards	Worsted Weight Yarn
51 (46.7m)	☐ Off-white
8 (7.4m)	▨ Heather gray
3 (2.8m)	▨ Medium sage
	⟋ Off-white Straight Stitch
	⟋ Heather gray Backstitch and Straight Stitch
	⟋ Medium sage Straight Stitch

	Bulky Weight Yarn
24 (22m)	▨ Mocha #210-125
6 (5.5m)	☐ Shaker #301
	⟋ Shaker #301 Backstitch
	● Attach ½-inch (1.3cm) button
	● Attach ¾-inch (1.9cm) button
	● Attach twine bow

Color numbers given are for Lion Brand Yarn Lion Suede bulky weight yarn Article #210 and Homespun bulky weight yarn Article #790.

Roof Side

Upper Birdhouse Side

Lower Birdhouse Top

Birdhouse Front

Lower Birdhouse Side

Birdhouse Assembly Diagram

Birdhouse Welcome Sign Side
4 holes x 19 holes
Cut 2

Upper Birdhouse Roof Side
4 holes x 10 holes
Cut 2

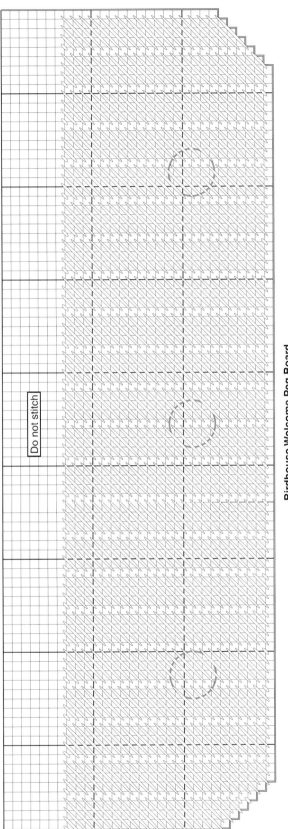

Birdhouse Welcome Peg Board
89 holes x 30 holes
Cut 1

Do not stitch

Birdhouse Welcome Sign Front
65 holes x 19 holes
Cut 1

Welcome Home Birdie

Open the tiny door on this stitched piece and fly home to your nest! Behind the door is a full house just waiting for someone to take roost. DESIGN BY GINA WOODS

Skill Level

Beginner

Size

8 inches W x 10¾ inches H (20.3cm x 27.3cm)

Materials

- 1 sheet 7-count plastic canvas
- Worsted weight yarn as listed in color key
- 6-strand embroidery floss as listed in color key
- #16 tapestry needle
- Small amount Patons Yarn Allure mink #04013 super bulky eyelash yarn from Spinrite Inc. (optional)
- Scrap red felt
- 7mm wood bead
- ¾-inch (1.9cm) plastic ring
- 4 inches (10.2cm) 26-gauge black wire
- Hand-sewing needle
- Tan sewing thread
- Short length ⅛-inch (3mm) dowel
- Hot-glue gun

Cutting & Stitching

1. Cut plastic canvas according to graphs (pages 94 and 95). Cut a ⅜-inch (1cm) heart from red felt; set aside.

2. Stitch and Overcast butterfly following graph, using 2 plies dark periwinkle to work Continental Stitches.

3. Stitch welcome piece following graph, using double strand light chartreuse to work Straight Stitches on foliage and working uncoded areas with Continental Stitches as follows: birdhouse with tan, foliage with chartreuse, sign with off-white. Overcast piece, leaving left edge of opening unstitched.

4. Overcast nest spacer. Stitch and Overcast remaining pieces following graphs, working uncoded background on nest with black Continental Stitches and leaving left edge of door unstitched.

5. When background stitching and Overcasting are completed, use dark brown floss to Backstitch detail on baby bird and black floss to Backstitch baby bird's legs and feet and to outline eggs in nest.

6. Work chartreuse and light chartreuse Straight Stitches on birdhouse and yellow-orange Straight Stitch for beak on baby bird.

7. Secure a 2-ply length of black floss on wrong side of butterfly. Where indicated on graph, wrap floss around center four or five times to form body.

8. For antennae, slip single ply of black floss under several threads at top of body. Tie ends in a knot at top, then trim antennae to desired length.

Assembly

1. Using sewing needle and tan thread, attach bead to door where indicated on graph. Using tan yarn, Whipstitch left edge of door to left edge of opening on birdhouse.

2. If desired, glue mink eyelash yarn to cover camel-colored area of nest. Glue nest spacer on front of nest, then center and glue nest assembly behind door of birdhouse.

3. Center bottom of plastic ring on top back of nest assembly. Attach with sewing needle and thread.

4. Glue heart to birdhouse where indicated on graph. Center and glue roof to top edge of birdhouse.

5. Insert 1 inch (2.5cm) of one end of wire under stitches on back of butterfly; bend end over to secure. Wrap wire two or three times around dowel approximately ½

inch (1.3cm) from butterfly.
Pull coils slightly to loosen.

6. Insert other end of wire under stitches on back of foliage where indicated with arrow. Bend end over to secure; trim excess.

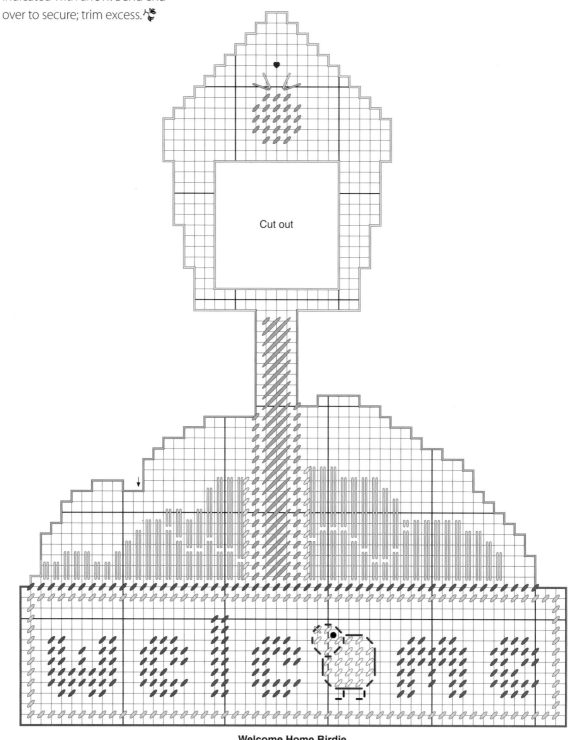

Welcome Home Birdie
53 holes x 67 holes
Cut 1

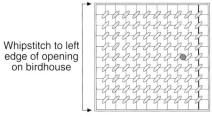

Whipstitch to left edge of opening on birdhouse

Welcome Home Birdie Door
11 holes x 10 holes
Cut 1

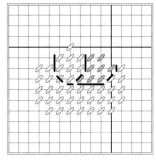

Welcome Home Birdie Nest
14 holes x 14 holes
Cut 1

Welcome Home Birdie Butterfly
4 holes x 4 holes
Cut 1

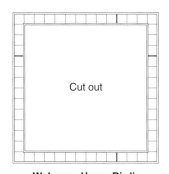

Cut out

**Welcome Home Birdie
Nest Spacer**
14 holes x 14 holes
Cut 1
Do not stitch

COLOR KEY	
Yards	**Worsted Weight Yarn**
10 (9.2m)	☐ Tan
10 (9.2m)	☐ Light chartreuse
7 (6.5m)	■ Dark brown
4 (3.7m)	▨ Medium brown
4 (3.7m)	▨ Bronze
3 (2.8m)	▨ Black
3 (2.8m)	☐ Light periwinkle
2 (1.9m)	☐ Camel
1 (1m)	☐ Yellow
1 (1m)	▨ Dark periwinkle (2 plies)
1 (1m)	☐ Light aqua
1 (1m)	▨ Dark aqua
10 (9.2m)	Uncoded areas on foliage are chartreuse Continental Stitches Uncoded areas on birdhouse are tan Continental Stitches
7 (6.5m)	Uncoded background on sign is off-white Continental Stitches Uncoded background on nest is black Continental Stitches
	⁄ Chartreuse Straight Stitch and Overcasting
	⁄ Light chartreuse Straight Stitch
1 (1m)	⁄ Yellow-orange Straight Stitch
	6-Strand Embroidery Floss
1 (1m)	✎ Black Backstitch and Straight Stitch
1 (1m)	✎ Dark brown Backstitch
	● Black French Knot
	● Attach bead
	♥ Attach heart

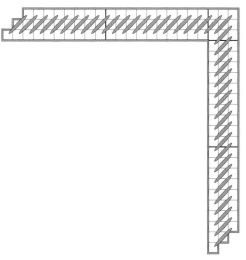

Welcome Home Birdie Roof
23 holes x 23 holes
Cut 1

Feathered Friends Door Decor

Pick between a mallard duck or majestic cardinal to greet your friends. DESIGNS BY NANCY DORMAN

Skill Level
Beginner

Size
Welcome Sign: 11⅝ inches W x 17 inches H (29.5cm x 43.2cm)
Cardinal: 6¾ inches W x 6¾ inches H (17.1cm x 17.1cm)
Mallard Duck: 7¾ inches W x 6¼ inches H (19.7cm x 15.9cm)

Materials
- 3 sheets 7-count plastic canvas
- Worsted weight yarn as listed in color key
- #16 tapestry needle
- 3 yards (2.8m) ¼-inch/7mm-wide ivory satin ribbon
- 4 inches (10.2cm) ¾-inch/1.9cm-wide hook-and-loop tape
- Hand-sewing needle
- Thread to match hook-and-loop tape
- Hot-glue gun

Project Note
The diamond, heart, flower, pentagon, square, star, triangle and inverted triangle symbols in the Color Key all designate Continental Stitches.

Sign
1. Cut letters and top and bottom trim from plastic canvas according to graphs (pages 99 and 100). Sign board (page 100) is one entire 70-hole x 90-hole sheet of plastic canvas.
2. Following project note and graphs throughout, stitch and Overcast trim and letter pieces. Stitch sign board, leaving four bars at top and bottom unworked. Overcast only side edges indicated, leaving edges along unworked areas unstitched.
3. Cut one ½ inch (1.3cm) length hook-and-loop tape. Separate tape sections. Place hook section 5¾ inches (14.6cm) from bottom edge on middle row of stitches. Using hand-sewing needle and thread, firmly sew tape in place.
4. Repeat with loop section of tape, firmly attaching to middle row of stitches 3⅛ inches (8cm) below top section.

5. Center and glue top trim to sign board, covering unstitched area and overlapping about one bar of stitching. Turn bottom trim so long straight edge is at the top. Glue in place, following instructions for top trim.
6. Using photo as a guide, tack letters in place below top trim with ivory yarn.
7. Make a multi-loop bow with ivory satin ribbon. Secure through hole on bottom trim.

Cardinal
1. Cut cardinal, flower and branch leaf pieces from plastic canvas according to graphs (pages 98 and 99), cutting out gray areas on cardinal piece.
2. Following project note and graphs throughout, stitch and Overcast pieces, working un-coded areas on cardinal with red Continental Stitches.
3. When background stitching is completed, work medium green Straight Stitches on leaves and straw French Knots on flowers.
4. Using photo as guide, sew leaves and flowers to branch with matching yarn.
5. Cut one ½ inch (1.3cm) length

hook-and-loop tape. Separate tape sections. Using hand-sewing needle and matching thread, firmly sew loop section to back of cardinal and hook section to back of branch and flowers to correspond with hook-and-loop tape on sign board.

Mallard Duck

1. Cut duck, cattail and cattail leaves from plastic canvas

according to graphs.

2. Following project note and graphs throughout, stitch and Overcast pieces, working uncoded area on duck with taupe Continental Stitches.

3. When background stitching is completed, work rust Straight Stitch for eye on duck.

4. Using photo as guide, sew cattail and leaves to back of duck with matching yarn.

5. Cut one ½ inch (1.3cm) length hook-and-loop tape. Separate tape sections. Using hand-sewing needle and matching thread, firmly sew loop section to back of cattail and leaves; sew hook section to back of duck to correspond with hook-and-loop tape on sign board.

Note: It may be necessary to trim loop section to fit behind cattail and leaves.

Small Flower
5 holes x 5 holes
Cut 1

Large Flower
7 holes x 7 holes
Cut 2

Branch Leaf
5 holes x 5 holes
Cut 5

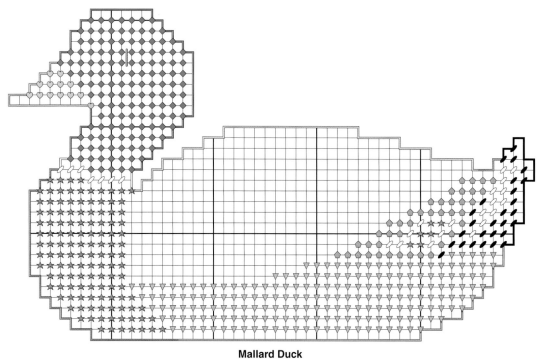

Mallard Duck
51 holes x 31 holes
Cut 1

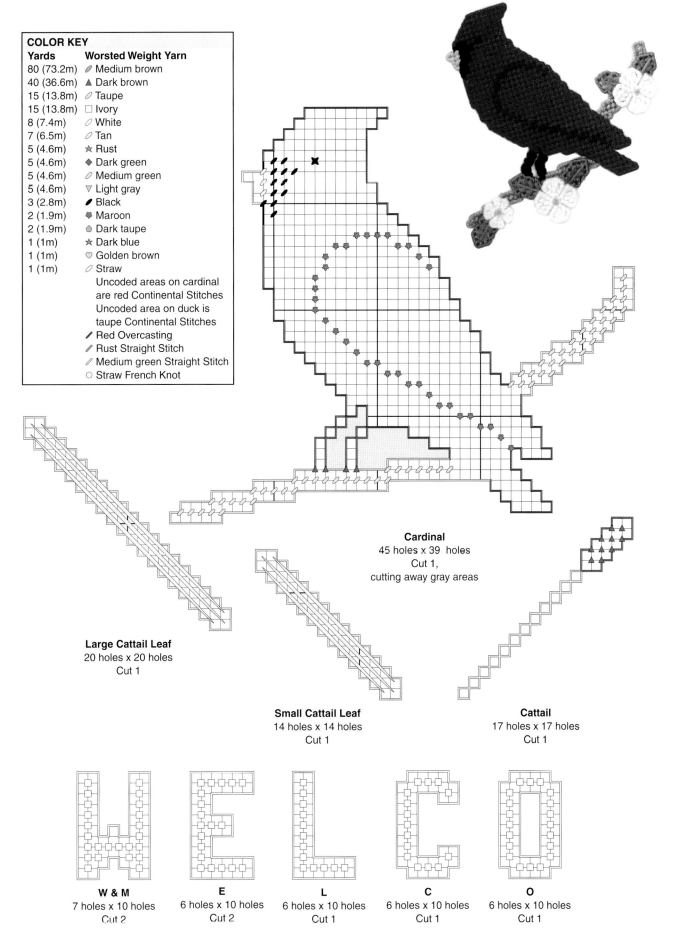

COLOR KEY

Yards	Worsted Weight Yarn
80 (73.2m)	⊘ Medium brown
40 (36.6m)	▲ Dark brown
15 (13.8m)	⊘ Taupe
15 (13.8m)	☐ Ivory
8 (7.4m)	⊘ White
7 (6.5m)	⊘ Tan
5 (4.6m)	★ Rust
5 (4.6m)	◆ Dark green
5 (4.6m)	⊘ Medium green
5 (4.6m)	▽ Light gray
3 (2.8m)	◣ Black
2 (1.9m)	✿ Maroon
2 (1.9m)	⬠ Dark taupe
1 (1m)	★ Dark blue
1 (1m)	♡ Golden brown
1 (1m)	⊘ Straw

Uncoded areas on cardinal
are red Continental Stitches
Uncoded area on duck is
taupe Continental Stitches
╱ Red Overcasting
╱ Rust Straight Stitch
⊘ Medium green Straight Stitch
○ Straw French Knot

Cardinal
45 holes x 39 holes
Cut 1,
cutting away gray areas

Large Cattail Leaf
20 holes x 20 holes
Cut 1

Small Cattail Leaf
14 holes x 14 holes
Cut 1

Cattail
17 holes x 17 holes
Cut 1

W & M
7 holes x 10 holes
Cut 2

E
6 holes x 10 holes
Cut 2

L
6 holes x 10 holes
Cut 1

C
6 holes x 10 holes
Cut 1

O
6 holes x 10 holes
Cut 1

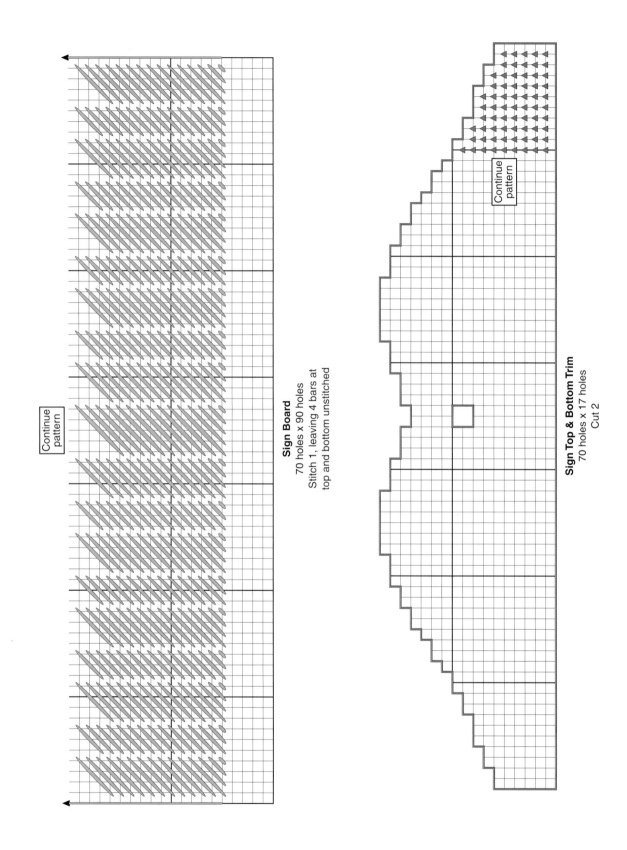

Continue
pattern

Sign Board
70 holes x 90 holes
Stitch 1, leaving 4 bars at
top and bottom unstitched

Continue
pattern

Sign Top & Bottom Trim
70 holes x 17 holes
Cut 2

Ladybug Doorstop

Keep your doors propped open during breezy days with this charming stop. A cement block or brick serves as the weight. DESIGN BY DEBRA ARCH

Skill Level
Intermediate

Size
7 inches W x 6½ inches H x 4 inches D (17.8cm x 16.5cm x 10.2cm), including buttons and beads

Materials
- 1 artist-sized sheet 7-count plastic canvas
- Uniek Needloft plastic canvas yarn as listed in color key
- #16 tapestry needle
- 20 (⅝-inch/1.6cm) round black low dome buttons
- 1 white chenille stem
- 30 (9 x 6mm) white pearl pony beads
- 2 black E beads
- Crescent-shaped landscape edging cement block or brick
- Hot-glue gun

Instructions
1. Cut plastic canvas according to graphs (pages 102 and 103), joining left and right halves of gusset before cutting as one piece. Back will remain unstitched.

2. Stitch front, gusset and base following graphs, working white Straight Stitches when background stitching is completed.

3. Whipstitch ends of gusset to side edges of base with red. Matching centers of both pieces, Whipstitch gusset and base to body front with red, white and black.

4. For antennae, thread ends of chenille stem from back to front through holes indicated with yellow dots; pull through and make ends even. Thread 14 beads on each end of stem, then bring ends down through holes indicated with blue dots. Twist ends together on back side to tighten and secure.

5. Insert cement block or brick in body, then Whipstitch body back in place.

6. For eyes, glue remaining two white pony beads with hole facing up to front where indicated on graph. For pupils, glue one black E bead in hole of each pony bead.

7. Glue buttons to body and gusset where indicated on graphs. 🐞

COLOR KEY

Yards	Plastic Canvas Yarn
33 (30.2m)	■ Black #00
44 (40.2m)	■ Red #01
10 (9.2m)	⁄ White #41 Straight Stitch
	● Attach black button
	● Attach pony bead for eye

Color numbers given are for Uniek Needloft plastic canvas yarn.

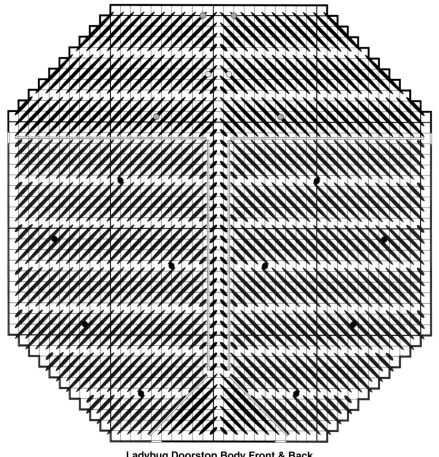

Ladybug Doorstop Body Front & Back
41 holes x 41 holes
Cut 2
Stitch front only

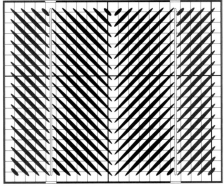

Ladybug Doorstop Body Base
21 holes x 17 holes
Cut 1

Middle Row
Do not repeat

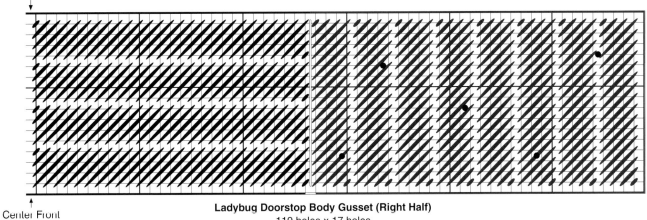

Center Front

Ladybug Doorstop Body Gusset (Right Half)
119 holes x 17 holes
Cut 1
Join with left half
before cutting as 1 piece

Middle Row
Do not repeat

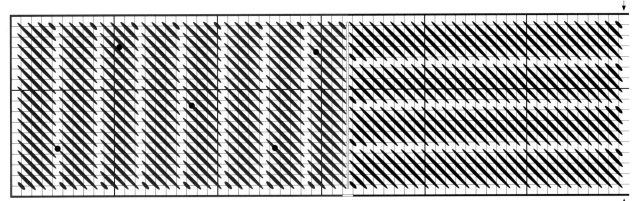

Ladybug Doorstop Body Gusset (Left Half)
119 holes x 17 holes
Cut 1
Join with right half
before cutting as 1 piece

Center Front

Garden Angel

Hang this sweet angel anywhere and she'll stand guard over your garden and plants. DESIGN BY TERRY RICIOLI

Skill Level

Intermediate

Size

11½ inches W x 12⅞ inches H (29.2cm x 32.7cm)

Materials

- 1 sheet clear 7-count plastic canvas
- 1 sheet white 7-count plastic canvas
- Uniek Needloft plastic canvas yarn as listed in color key
- #16 tapestry needle
- Buttons: flowers, ladybugs, garden signs, garden tools as desired
- 10mm letter beads to spell "WELCOME"
- 8 inches (20.3cm) One & Only Creations Beautiful Braids medium brown #300 doll hair
- 6 inches (15.2cm) 2¼-inch/56mm-wide multicolored floral craft ribbon
- Hot-glue gun

Cutting & Stitching

1. Following graphs throughout (pages 106 and 109), cut angel front from clear and angel back from white plastic canvas. Cut remaining pieces from clear plastic canvas. Angel back and hat back will remain unstitched.

2. Stitch and Overcast sign. Stitch and Overcast feet and pockets, reversing one of each before stitching.

3. Stitch and Overcast one leaf wing as graphed; working uncoded areas with fern Continental Stitches. Reverse remaining leaf wing and work stitches in reverse.

4. Stitch angel front following graph, working uncoded background on face, neck and hands with pale peach Continental Stitches. Work black Straight Stitches and lavender Backstitches on face when background stitching is completed. Overcast bottom edge.

5. Whipstitch body front and back together, leaving bottom open.

6. Stitch basket front and hat pieces following graphs, leaving area on hat back unworked as indicated.

7. With right sides facing front, Whipstitch hat front and back together around side and top edges from dot to dot. Overcast remaining edges.

8. Whipstitch basket front and back together around side and bottom edges from dot to dot. Overcast remaining edges.

Final Assembly

1. Using photo as a guide throughout final assembly, glue feet inside jumper to body front, placing one foot higher than the other.

2. Using camel yarn, attach beads to sign where indicated on graph. For hanger, cut 10-inch (25.4cm) length camel yarn. Thread ends from back to front through holes indicated on sign graph. Adjust length as desired, then knot ends in front.

3. Place hanger over one hand; glue to front and back of hand. Glue basket handle to back of other hand.

4. Unbraid hair and glue to head, arranging as desired.

5. Glue leaf wings to back of shoulders, hat to head and straight edges of pockets to jumper where indicated with red lines.

6. Cut one 2¼-inch (5.7cm) square from ribbon; fold in half diagonally two times, then glue inside one pocket.

7. Cut remaining ribbon in half length-wise. Fold one length in a strip and glue to hat for hatband, gluing ends on back side. Fold remaining length as desired for tails; glue to back left side of hat at hatband, trimming as necessary.

8. Glue buttons to hat, sign, wings, basket and angel as desired.

9. Hang as desired. 🕊

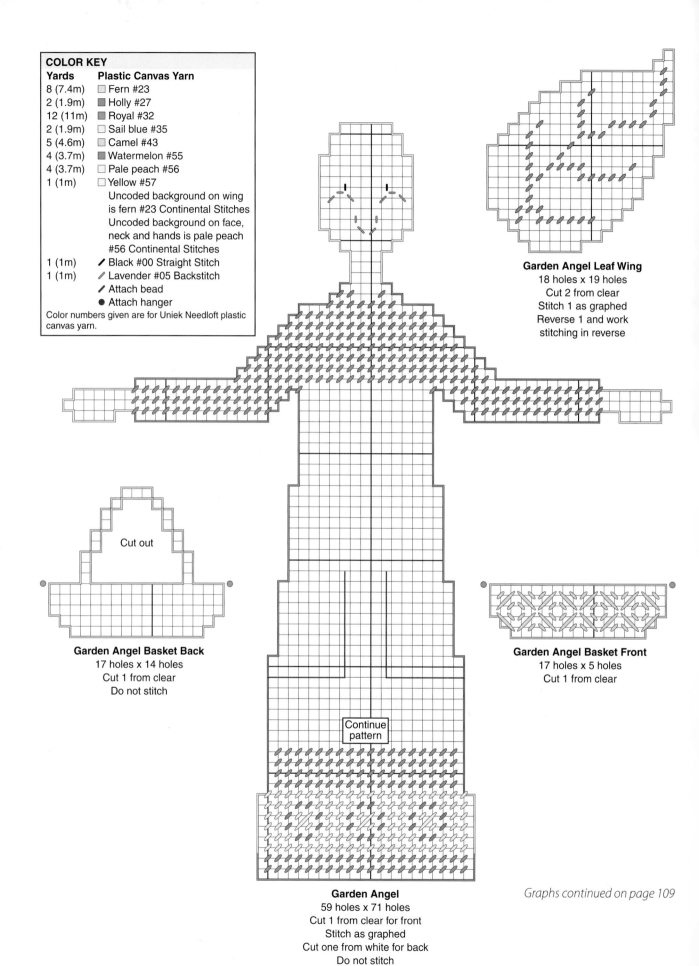

COLOR KEY

Yards	Plastic Canvas Yarn
8 (7.4m)	☐ Fern #23
2 (1.9m)	▨ Holly #27
12 (11m)	▨ Royal #32
2 (1.9m)	☐ Sail blue #35
5 (4.6m)	☐ Camel #43
4 (3.7m)	▨ Watermelon #55
4 (3.7m)	☐ Pale peach #56
1 (1m)	☐ Yellow #57

Uncoded background on wing
is fern #23 Continental Stitches
Uncoded background on face,
neck and hands is pale peach
#56 Continental Stitches

1 (1m)	✎ Black #00 Straight Stitch
1 (1m)	✎ Lavender #05 Backstitch
	✎ Attach bead
	● Attach hanger

Color numbers given are for Uniek Needloft plastic
canvas yarn.

Garden Angel Leaf Wing
18 holes x 19 holes
Cut 2 from clear
Stitch 1 as graphed
Reverse 1 and work
stitching in reverse

Cut out

Garden Angel Basket Back
17 holes x 14 holes
Cut 1 from clear
Do not stitch

Continue
pattern

Garden Angel Basket Front
17 holes x 5 holes
Cut 1 from clear

Garden Angel
59 holes x 71 holes
Cut 1 from clear for front
Stitch as graphed
Cut one from white for back
Do not stitch

Graphs continued on page 109

Sunbonnet Cheer

Cheer a friend with a greeting from everyone's favorite sunbonnet-wearing duo! DESIGN BY ALIDA MACOR

Skill Level
Intermediate

Size
13½ inches W x 9½ inches H (34.3cm x 24.1cm)

Materials
- 1 sheet stiff 7-count plastic canvas
- Uniek Needloft plastic canvas yarn as listed in color key
- Worsted weight yarn as listed in color key
- Uniek Needloft metallic craft cord as listed in color key
- #16 tapestry needle
- 9 inches (22.9cm) ⅛-inch/
- 3mm-wide pink satin ribbon
- 9 inches (22.9cm) ⅛-inch/ 3mm-wide blue satin ribbon
- 8 inches (20.3cm) gold chain by the yard
- Needle-nose pliers
- Hot-glue gun

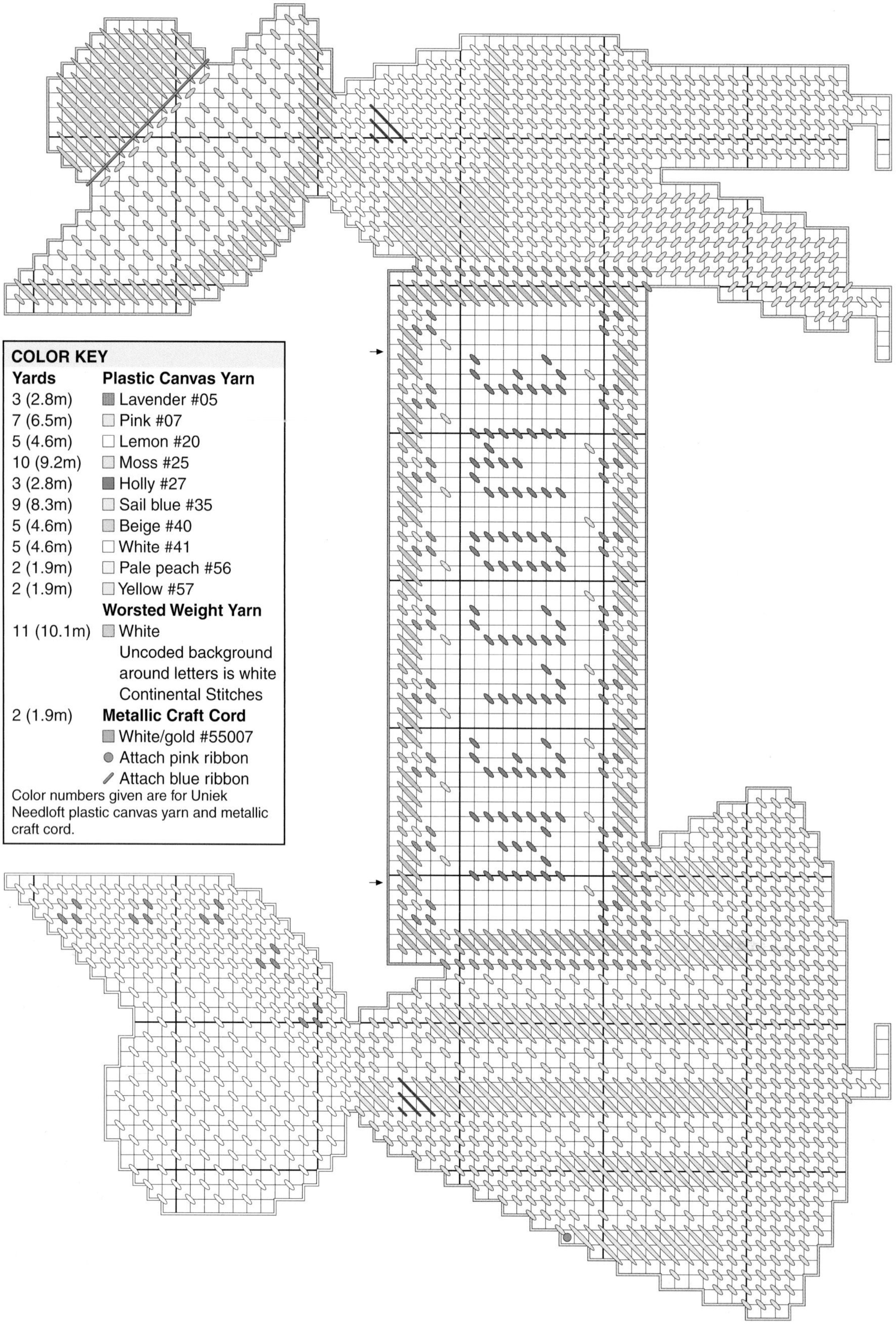

COLOR KEY

Yards	Plastic Canvas Yarn
3 (2.8m)	Lavender #05
7 (6.5m)	Pink #07
5 (4.6m)	Lemon #20
10 (9.2m)	Moss #25
3 (2.8m)	Holly #27
9 (8.3m)	Sail blue #35
5 (4.6m)	Beige #40
5 (4.6m)	White #41
2 (1.9m)	Pale peach #56
2 (1.9m)	Yellow #57

	Worsted Weight Yarn
11 (10.1m)	White
	Uncoded background around letters is white Continental Stitches

	Metallic Craft Cord
2 (1.9m)	White/gold #55007
	Attach pink ribbon
	Attach blue ribbon

Color numbers given are for Uniek Needloft plastic canvas yarn and metallic craft cord.

Sunbonnet Cheer Motif
89 holes x 62 holes
Cut 1

Instructions

1. Cut plastic canvas according to graphs.

2. Stitch and Overcast pieces following graphs, leaving areas indicated with red lines unworked and working uncoded background on sign with white worsted weight yarn Continental Stitches. Conceal yarn ends behind "open weave" portions on bonnet, apron and hat.

3. Matching red lines, attach arms to corresponding shoulders, following Slanted Gobelin Stitch pattern on arms. Glue hands to sign (see photo).

4. Thread pink ribbon through hole indicated at back of Sue's apron; tie in a knot. If desired, secure knot with glue.

5. Attach blue ribbon to Bill's hat where indicated on graph, overlapping and gluing ends on back side.

6. For hanger, use needle-nose pliers to attach chain to sign where indicated at arrows.

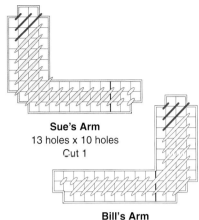

Sue's Arm
13 holes x 10 holes
Cut 1

Bill's Arm
14 holes x 10 holes
Cut 1

Garden Angel

Continued from page 106

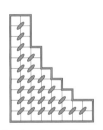

Garden Angel Pocket
8 holes x 10 holes
Cut 2, reverse 1, from clear

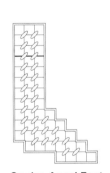

Garden Angel Foot
8 holes x 13 holes
Cut 2, reverse 1, from clear

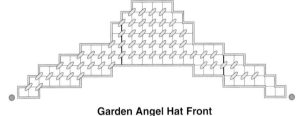

Garden Angel Hat Front
26 holes x 9 holes
Cut 1 from clear

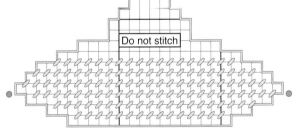

Do not stitch

Garden Angel Hat Back
26 holes x 12 holes
Cut 1 from clear

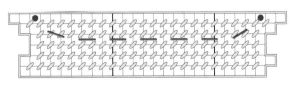

Garden Angel Sign
27 holes x 6 holes
Cut 1 from clear

COLOR KEY

Yards	Plastic Canvas Yarn
8 (7.4m)	☐ Fern #23
2 (1.9m)	■ Holly #27
12 (11m)	■ Royal #32
2 (1.9m)	☐ Sail blue #35
5 (4.6m)	☐ Camel #43
4 (3.7m)	▩ Watermelon #55
4 (3.7m)	☐ Pale peach #56
1 (1m)	☐ Yellow #57
	Uncoded background on wing is fern #23 Continental Stitches
	Uncoded background on face, neck and hands is pale peach #56 Continental Stitches
1 (1m)	✦ Black #00 Straight Stitch
1 (1m)	✦ Lavender #05 Backstitch
	✦ Attach bead
	● Attach hanger

Color numbers given are for Uniek Needloft plastic canvas yarn.

Daisy Flyswatter

Hang this swatter on or near your chair and keep pesky flies at bay. DESIGN BY NANCY DORMAN

Skill Level
Beginner

Size
4⅝ inches W x 6⅜ inches H (11.7cm x 16.2cm), excluding handle

Materials
- 1 sheet blue 7-count plastic canvas
- Worsted weight yarn as listed in color key
- #16 tapestry needle
- Wire-handle flyswatter

Instructions

1. Cut front and back from plastic canvas according to graph (page 115). Back will remain unstitched.

2. Stitch front following graph, working black Backstitches while stitching bee. Try not to pass yarn too often behind unstitched areas.

3. Using a double strand white, Overcast top edges of front and back pieces from A to B. Place back piece behind front, matching edges, then Whipstitch around right side and bottom from B to C.

4. Insert flyswatter and continue Whipstitching from C to A.

Nautical Doorstop

Add your favorite nautical embellishments, such as shells or a tiny bird, to complete this majestic lighthouse. DESIGN BY TERRY RICIOLI

Skill Level
Intermediate

Size
8 inches W x 17¾ inches H x 3⅝ inches D (20.3cm x 45cm x 9.2cm)

Materials
- 2 sheets clear 7-count plastic canvas
- Strip red 7-count plastic canvas
- 6-inch Uniek QuickShape plastic canvas radial circle
- Uniek Needloft plastic canvas yarn as listed in color key
- #16 tapestry needle
- Zip-close plastic bag
- Rocks or beans for weight
- Few small rocks for embellishment
- Metal bookend (optional)
- Hot-glue gun

Cutting & Stitching

1. Cut lighthouse front, lighthouse back, base, light room window, light room back and roof pieces from clear plastic canvas according to graphs (this page and pages 113, 114 and 115). Lighthouse back and light back will remain unstitched.

2. Cut railing from red plastic canvas following graph, carefully cutting out 13 holes. Railing will remain unstitched.

3. Cut observation deck from 6-inch plastic canvas radial circle, cutting away gray area. Do not cut away blue area.

4. Stitch pieces following graphs, leaving area indicated on base and shaded blue area on deck unworked.

5. Overcast top and bottom edges of lighthouse front; Overcast top and bottom edges of light pieces.

Assembly

1. Whipstitch lighthouse front to lighthouse back along side edges. Center lighthouse on base over unstitched area, then Whipstitch lighthouse back to back edge of base where indicated. Overcast remaining edges of base.

2. Whipstitch bottom edge of railing to curved edge of observation deck. Center deck on top edge of lighthouse, then Whipstitch deck to top edge of lighthouse back, Overcasting remaining edges of deck while Whipstitching. Glue top edge of lighthouse to bottom of deck.

3. Whipstitch light room windows together, making a strip of three pieces, then Whipstitch the end window pieces to side edges of light room back.

4. Whipstitch three roof pieces together along side edges, then Whipstitch roof pieces on ends to light room back, matching yellow dots. Overcast remaining roof edges.

5. Center light room assembly over unstitched area on deck, aligning back edges; glue in place.

6. Fill zip-close plastic bag with rocks or beans. Tip lighthouse back at base and place bag inside lighthouse. Glue front edge of lighthouse to base.

7. If desired, glue metal bookend to back and base for more stability.

8. Glue small rocks to base around lighthouse.

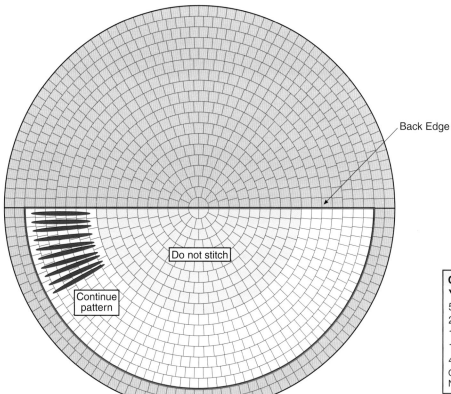

Back Edge

Do not stitch

Continue pattern

Lighthouse Observation Deck
Cut 1 from 6-inch radial circle,
cutting away gray area
Do not cut away blue area

Light Room Window
12 holes x 15 holes
Cut 3 from clear

COLOR KEY		
Yards	**Plastic Canvas Yarn**	
50 (45.7m)	■ Christmas red #02	
20 (18.3m)	■ Cinnamon #14	
10 (9.2m)	□ Sail blue #35	
10 (9.2m)	▨ Gray #38	
40 (36.6m)	□ White #41	

Color numbers given are for Uniek Needloft plastic canvas yarn.

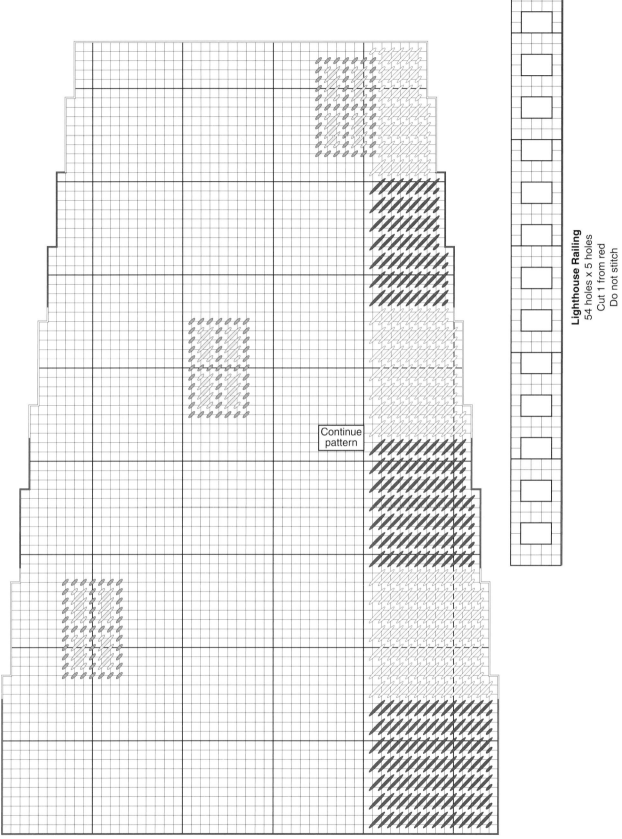

Lighthouse Railing
54 holes x 5 holes
Cut 1 from red
Do not stitch

Continue pattern

Lighthouse Front
55 holes x 85 holes
Cut 1 from clear

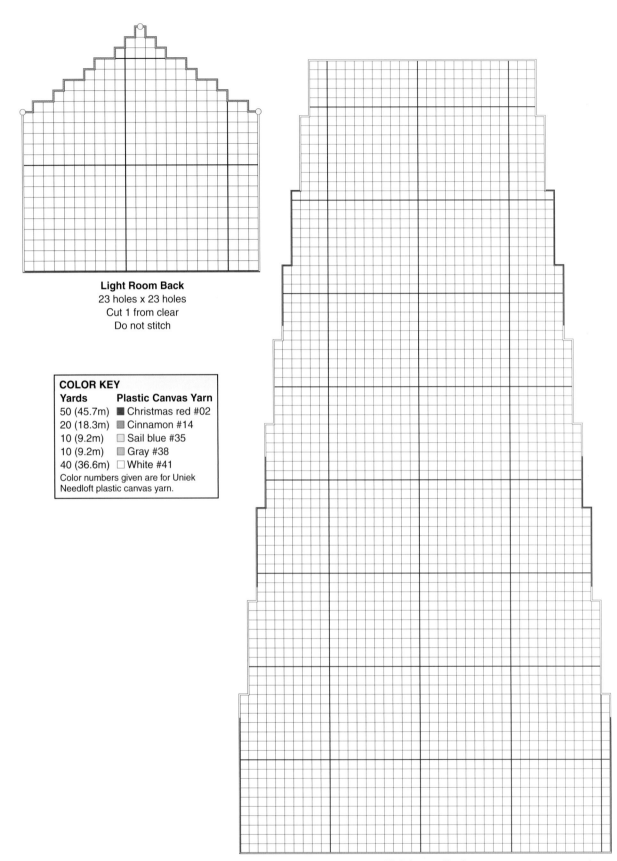

Light Room Back
23 holes x 23 holes
Cut 1 from clear
Do not stitch

COLOR KEY

Yards		Plastic Canvas Yarn
50 (45.7m)	■	Christmas red #02
20 (18.3m)	■	Cinnamon #14
10 (9.2m)	□	Sail blue #35
10 (9.2m)	■	Gray #38
40 (36.6m)	□	White #41

Color numbers given are for Uniek
Needloft plastic canvas yarn.

Lighthouse Back
41 holes x 85 holes
Cut 1 from clear
Do not stitch

Whipstitch to lighthouse back

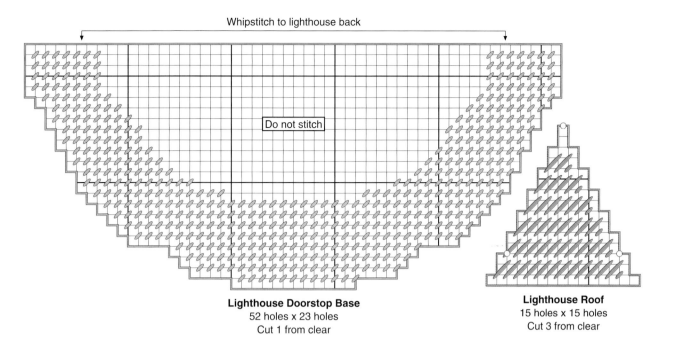

Do not stitch

Lighthouse Doorstop Base
52 holes x 23 holes
Cut 1 from clear

Lighthouse Roof
15 holes x 15 holes
Cut 3 from clear

Flyswatter

Continued from page 110

COLOR KEY

Yards	Worsted Weight Yarn
10 (9.2m)	☐ White
2 (1.9m)	▨ Green
1 (1m)	■ Black
1 (1m)	☐ Yellow
	✏ Black Backstitch

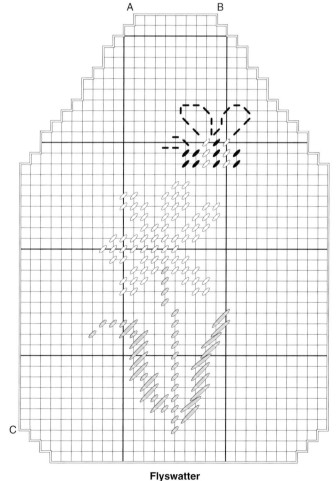

Flyswatter
30 holes x 42 holes
Cut 2, stitch 1

Wind Chimes, Spinners & Mobiles

Catch a breeze year-round with this chapter filled with whimsical spinners and wind chimes stitched in a variety of motifs. There's sure to be something you'll love!

Flip-Flop Mobile

Just as fun as a day at the beach, this mobile will delight the summer lover in you. DESIGN BY TERRY RICIOLI

Skill Level
Beginner

Size
5 inches W x 12½ inches L (12.7cm x 31.8cm) when hanging

Materials
- 1 sheet 7-count plastic canvas
- 2 (5-inch) Uniek QuickShape plastic canvas stars
- Uniek Needloft plastic canvas yarn as listed in color key
- #16 tapestry needle
- Assorted E beads in coordinating colors
- Assorted medium beads in coordinating colors
- 11 gold or silver crimp beads
- 2⅓ yards (2.1m) flexible beading wire
- 5 (8-inch/20.3cm) lengths 24-gauge gold wire
- Crimp pliers
- Wire cutter
- Hot-glue gun

Cutting & Stitching

1. Cut 10 sandals from plastic canvas and 2 flowers from stars following graphs (page 120), cutting away gray areas on stars.

2. Stitch flowers following graph. Whipstitch wrong sides together with bright blue.

3. Stitch flip-flop fronts following graphs, working uncoded areas on C front with eggshell and uncoded areas on E front with pink.

4. Stitch flip-flop backs with Continental Stitches as follows: A with fern, B with yellow, C with bittersweet, D with bright blue and E with watermelon.

Assembly

1. For each flip-flop, fold one length gold wire in half. Thread ends from back to front through holes indicated on front pieces at thong attachment. Using coordinating colors through step 2, thread on three E beads over both wires.

2. Separate wires and add one E bead to each wire, then alternate medium beads with E beads until strap attachment is reached.

Thread wire from front to back at these points and adjust beads. Twist wires together on back side and flatten to back. Trim as needed.

3. Whipstitch wrong sides of corresponding fronts and backs together following graphs.

4. Cut five 12-inch (30.5cm) lengths flexible beading wire for connecting wire. For each wire, thread crimp bead and E bead on one end. Thread end through hole indicated on flip-flop, then back through E bead and crimp bead; tighten and crimp.

5. Thread on 5–6 inches (12.7–15.2cm) of assorted beads, then add another crimp bead and E bead. Thread wire up, then down through holes indicated on flower, then back through E bead and crimp bead. Pull up wire and crimp bead. **Note:** *Use needle as needed to push wire through holes on flower.*

6. For hanger, using desired length of remaining beading wire, thread ends up through holes indicated. Add beads as desired. Thread both ends through crimp bead; tighten wire and crimp bead. Trim wire ends.

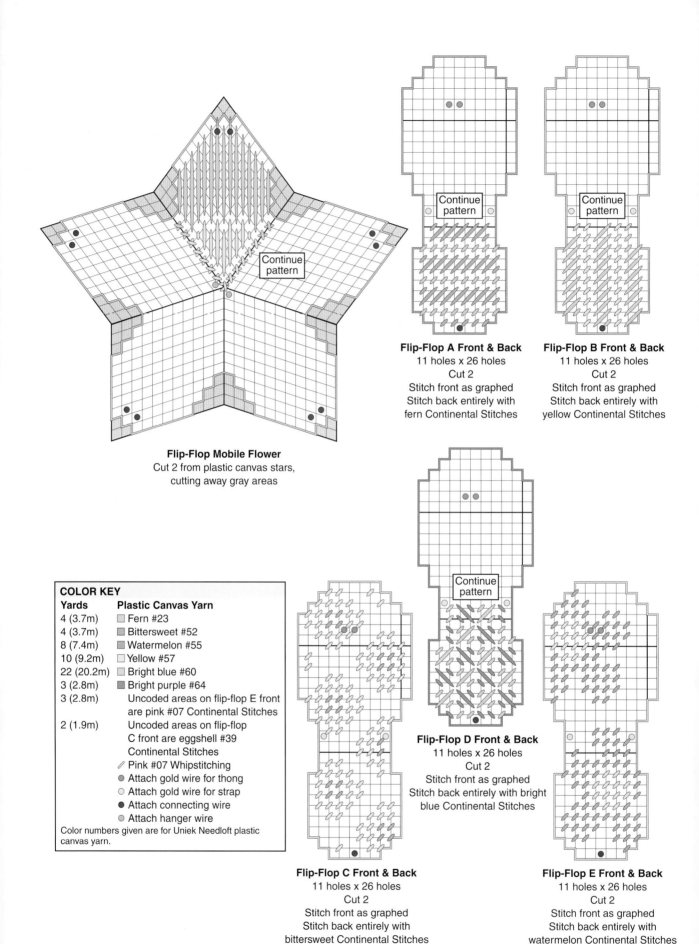

Flip-Flop Mobile Flower
Cut 2 from plastic canvas stars,
cutting away gray areas

Flip-Flop A Front & Back
11 holes x 26 holes
Cut 2
Stitch front as graphed
Stitch back entirely with
fern Continental Stitches

Flip-Flop B Front & Back
11 holes x 26 holes
Cut 2
Stitch front as graphed
Stitch back entirely with
yellow Continental Stitches

Flip-Flop D Front & Back
11 holes x 26 holes
Cut 2
Stitch front as graphed
Stitch back entirely with bright
blue Continental Stitches

COLOR KEY

Yards	Plastic Canvas Yarn
4 (3.7m)	☐ Fern #23
4 (3.7m)	◼ Bittersweet #52
8 (7.4m)	◼ Watermelon #55
10 (9.2m)	☐ Yellow #57
22 (20.2m)	☐ Bright blue #60
3 (2.8m)	◼ Bright purple #64
3 (2.8m)	Uncoded areas on flip-flop E front are pink #07 Continental Stitches
2 (1.9m)	Uncoded areas on flip-flop C front are eggshell #39 Continental Stitches
	╱ Pink #07 Whipstitching
	● Attach gold wire for thong
	○ Attach gold wire for strap
	● Attach connecting wire
	○ Attach hanger wire

Color numbers given are for Uniek Needloft plastic canvas yarn.

Flip-Flop C Front & Back
11 holes x 26 holes
Cut 2
Stitch front as graphed
Stitch back entirely with
bittersweet Continental Stitches

Flip-Flop E Front & Back
11 holes x 26 holes
Cut 2
Stitch front as graphed
Stitch back entirely with
watermelon Continental Stitches

A Garden Is Fun

Hang these delightful danglers from a tree branch or porch hook and watch the party fun begin. Select a party favor of your choice and tie onto the design with ribbon. DESIGN BY GINA WOODS

Skill Level
Beginner

Size
9⅜ inches W x 8¼ inches L (23.8cm x 21cm), excluding party favors and hanger

Materials
- 1 sheet stiff 7-count plastic canvas
- 9½-inch (24.1cm) plastic canvas radial circle
- Worsted weight yarn as listed in color key
- 6-strand embroidery floss as listed in color key
- #16 tapestry needle
- 5mm black pompom
- 24 inches (61cm) ¼-inch/ 7mm-wide royal blue satin ribbon
- 7 (15-inch/38.1cm) lengths ⅛-inch/3mm-wide lavender satin ribbon
- 7 bubble wands (or party favors of choice)
- ½-inch/1.3cm-diameter dowel
- Hot-glue gun

Instructions
1. Cut back, sign and ladybug from stiff plastic canvas; cut rainbow from plastic canvas radial circle following graphs (pages 123 and 124), cutting away blue graph lines in hanger tabs along bottom of sign and gray area on circle.

2. Continental Stitch and Overcast rainbow following graph, working two stitches per hole only when necessary.

3. Stitch and Overcast remaining pieces following graphs, working uncoded background on sign with white Continental Stitches and uncoded areas with white backgrounds on back with royal blue Continental Stitches. Uncoded area shaded with pale yellow will remain unstitched.

4. When background stitching is completed, work Backstitches, Straight Stitches, Lazy Daisy Stitches and French Knots as graphed.

5. Using photo as a guide through step 6, glue sign over unstitched portion of back, matching side and bottom edges and allowing hanger loops to extend below bottom edge.

6. Center and glue rainbow to top portion of background piece so bottom straight edges of rainbow meet top edges of sign.

7. Glue pompom to ladybug where indicated, then glue ladybug at top edge of sign, so Backstitches for antennae on far left leaf appear to be coming out of pompom head.

Finishing
1. Thread royal blue ribbon through several stitches at top back side of back piece; make tails even. Tie ends together in a bow to form a loop for hanging.

2. Thread one lavender ribbon through each hanging loop at bottom of sign, making ends even. For each ribbon, tie a double knot around dowel immediately below hanging loop to make loops consistent in size.

3. Tie bubble wand or party favor in place with a bow below ribbon loop; trim ends as desired. ***Note:*** *Leave ribbon long enough to retie another favor in place when one has been chosen.* ✒

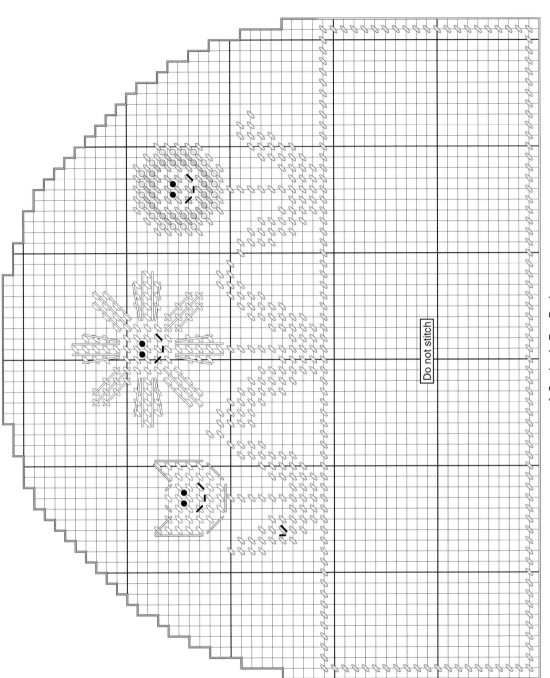

A Garden Is Fun Back
62 holes x 52 holes
Cut 1

Do not stitch

COLOR KEY

Yards	Worsted Weight Yarn
30 (27.5m)	☐ White
20 (18.3m)	☐ Lavender
14 (12.9m)	☐ Bright green
8 (7.4m)	☐ Medium dusty rose
7 (6.5m)	☐ Light aqua
5 (4.6m)	☐ Pale yellow
5 (4.6m)	☐ Light peach
2 (1.9m)	☐ Orange
1 (1m)	☐ Bright yellow
1 (1m)	☐ Yellow-orange
1 (1m)	■ Red
	Uncoded areas on back with white backgrounds are royal blue Continental Stitches
	Uncoded background on sign is white Continental Stitches
╱	Royal blue Straight Stitch and Overcasting
╱	White Straight Stitch
╱	Lavender Straight Stitch
⊘	Bright green Lazy Daisy Stitch
◉	Orange French Knot
○	Medium dusty rose French Knot
	6-Strand Embroidery Floss
3 (2.8m)	╱ Medium blue Backstitch and Straight Stitch
2 (1.9m)	╱ Black Backstitch
	● Black French Knot

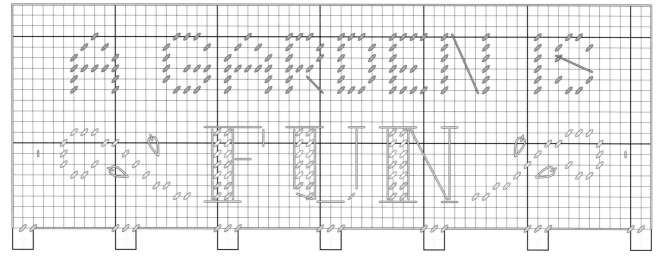

A Garden Is Fun Sign
62 holes x 23 holes
Cut 1,
cutting away blue graph lines

Attach pompom

A Garden Is Fun Ladybug
4 holes x 2 holes
Cut 1

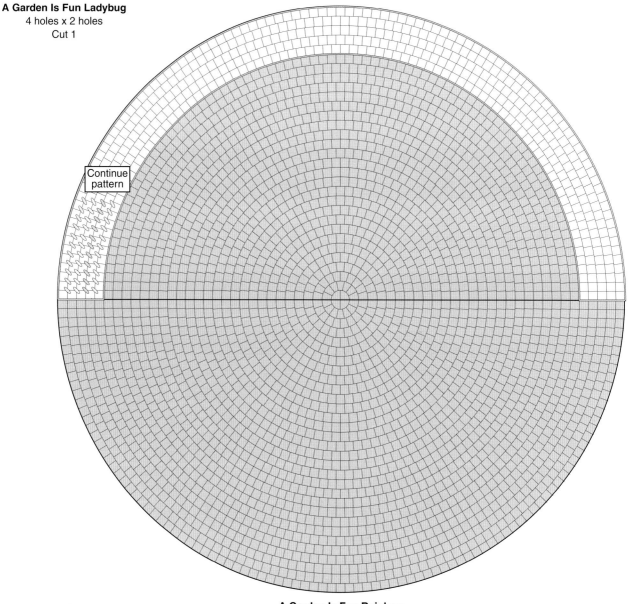

Continue pattern

A Garden Is Fun Rainbow
Cut 1 from radial circle,
cutting away gray area

Star Pride Forever

Red, white and blue pride abounds in this delightful piece, featuring stitched plastic canvas swirls. DESIGN BY ANGIE ARICKX

Skill Level
Intermediate

Size
7¾ inches W x 19½ inches L
(19.7cm x 49.5cm)
when hanging

Materials
- 4 (5-inch) Uniek QuickShape plastic canvas stars
- Coats & Clark Red Heart Super Saver worsted weight yarn Art. E300 as listed in color key
- #16 tapestry needle
- 1½-inch (3.8cm) white bear ornament
- 12 inches (30.5cm) Uniek Needloft white #55043 solid craft cord
- 5-inch Uniek gold-finish wire star shape #UCW0N02
- 24 inches (61cm) 12-pound nylon fishing line
- Hot-glue gun

Instructions
1. Cut stars according to graphs (this page and page 126), cutting away gray areas.
2. Stitch and Overcast stars following graphs as follows: one large star with burgundy and one with soft navy; two medium stars with white and two with burgundy; one small star with soft navy and one with burgundy.

3. Using photo as a guide through step 7, invert the two burgundy medium stars and place wrong sides together with gold wire star sandwiched between (see Fig. 1).

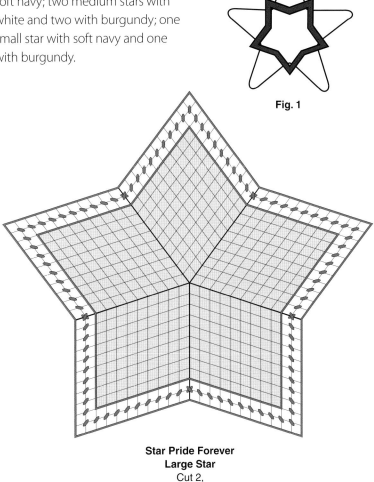

Fig. 1

Star Pride Forever
Large Star
Cut 2,
cutting away gray area
Stitch 1 as graphed
Stitch 1 with burgundy

Glue burgundy stars together at each outer and inner point.

4. Cut fishing line in half. Place remaining stars in two groups of three as follows: large soft navy, medium white, small burgundy and large burgundy, medium white, small soft navy.

5. Thread lengths of fishing line up through stitches on wrong side of each group of stars, securing first on a small star and ending with a large star (see Fig. 2). Tie loose ends of each fishing line to bottom points of gold wire star, staggering lengths as desired.

Fig. 2

6. Cut off knot from bear's hanging loop and thread lines through bottom hole of inverted burgundy stars; knot off.

7. Attach white craft cord to top of gold wire star with a Lark's Head Knot. Tie ends together in a knot at desired length to form a loop for hanging. ✂

COLOR KEY

Yards	Worsted Weight Yarn
5 (4.6m)	☐ White #311
10 (9.2m)	■ Burgundy #376
5 (4.6m)	▨ Soft navy #387

Color numbers given are for Coats & Clark Red Heart Super Saver worsted weight yarn Art. E300.

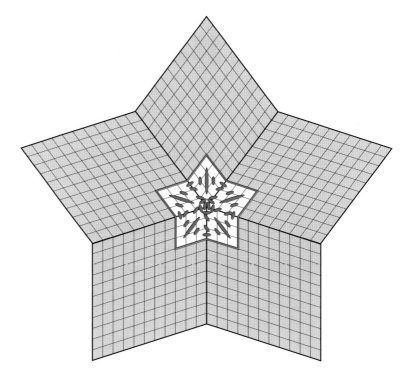

Star Pride Forever
Small Star
Cut 2,
cutting away gray area
Stitch 1 as graphed
Stitch 1 with burgundy

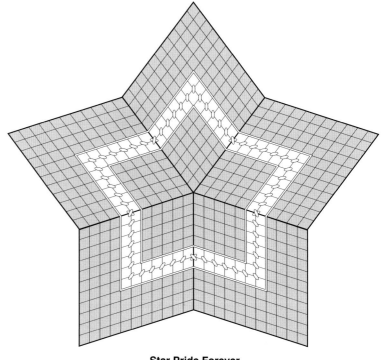

Star Pride Forever
Medium Star
Cut 4,
cutting away gray areas
Stitch 2 as graphed
Stitch 2 with burgundy

Patriotic Swirls

Red, white and blue pride abounds in this delightful piece, featuring stitched plastic canvas swirls. DESIGN BY ANGIE ARICKX

Skill Level
Intermediate

Size
7½ inches W x 33½ inches L (19.1cm x 85.1cm) when hanging

Materials
- 1 sheet 7-count plastic canvas
- 2 (5-inch) Uniek QuickShape plastic canvas stars
- Coats & Clark Red Heart Super Saver worsted weight yarn Art. E300 as listed in color key
- #16 tapestry needle
- 1 yard (1m) Uniek Needloft white #55043 solid craft cord

Instructions

1. Cut one swirl from plastic canvas according to graph.

2. Stitch and Overcast swirl following graph, working uncoded areas with white Continental Stitches. Stitch two stars following graph.

3. Thread white craft cord through hole indicated on swirl graph; make ends even and knot just above edge of canvas. Make a second knot about 2 inches (5.1cm) above first knot.

4. Place cord lengths together between stars, positioning second knot at center bottom edge of star at yellow dot. Using white, Whipstitch wrong sides of stars together, allowing cord lengths to exit star at yellow dots at star top.

5. Tie ends of cord together in a knot at desired length to form a loop for hanging. Trim ends as needed. ✄

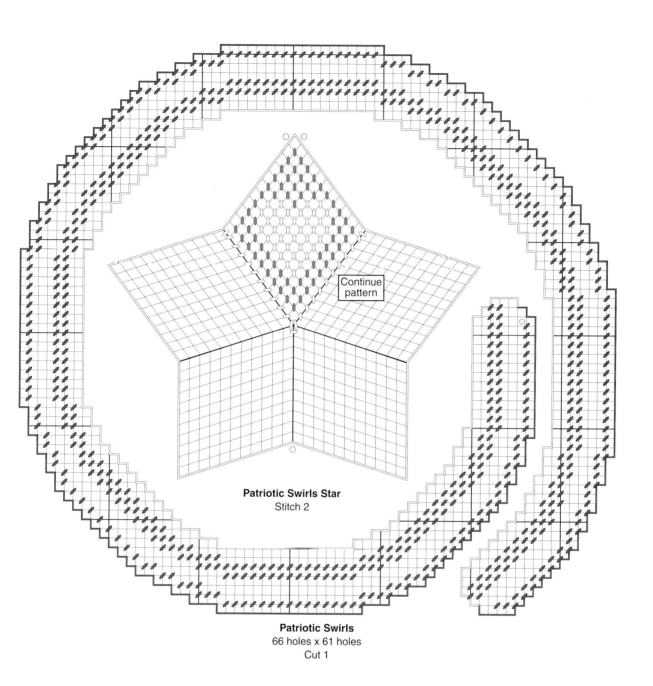

Patriotic Swirls Star
Stitch 2

Continue pattern

Patriotic Swirls
66 holes x 61 holes
Cut 1

COLOR KEY	
Yards	**Worsted Weight Yarn**
22 (20.2m)	☐ White #311
14 (12.9m)	■ Burgundy #376
12 (11m)	▨ Soft navy #387
	Uncoded areas on swirl are white #311 Continental Stitches
	○ Attach white craft cord

Color numbers given are for Coats & Clark Red Heart Super Saver worsted weight yarn Art. E300.

Time for a Picnic

Let all your friends know when the party begins with a picnic-inspired wind spinner embellished with ribbon. DESIGN BY PATRICIA KLESH

Skill Level

Beginner

Size

7⅜ inches W x 16 inches L (18.7cm x 40.6cm) when hanging

Materials

- 1 sheet 7-count plastic canvas
- Worsted weight yarn as listed in color key
- #16 tapestry needle
- 2 yards (1.9m) ⅜ -inch/ 9mm-wide red and white gingham ribbon
- 4 (¼-inch/0.6cm) brass brads/paper fasteners
- 18 inches (45.7cm) fishing line
- Black fine-tip permanent marker
- Tiny pieces stiff white paper
- Hot-glue gun

Instructions

1. Cut plastic canvas according to graphs.

2. Stitch and Overcast handles, chip bags, cola cans and cupcakes following graphs. Stitch basket pieces following graphs. Overcast bottom edges from blue dot to blue dot.

3. Cut ribbon in nine 8-inch (20.3cm) lengths. Glue side by side to wrong side of one basket piece about four bars from bottom edge, keeping edges free of glue.

4. With wrong sides facing, Whipstitch top edges of basket pieces together. Insert one brad/ paper fastener into one handle end

Picnic Basket
34 holes x 20 holes
Cut 2

COLOR KEY	
Yards	**Worsted Weight Yarn**
25 (22.9m)	☐ Tan
2 (1.9m)	☐ Turquoise
1 (1m)	■ Red
1 (1m)	☐ Light yellow
1 (1m)	☐ Yellow
1 (1m)	■ Brown
	● Attach brad/paper fastener
	● Attach fishing line

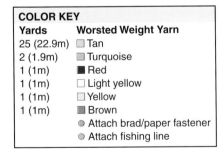

Picnic Basket Handle
44 holes x 3 holes
Cut 2

and basket where indicated on graphs.

5. Bring handle over top edge and insert through corresponding holes of handle and basket on other side. Repeat with second handle.

6. Whipstitch sides of basket together. Apply small amount of glue over ribbon inside basket and adhere to remaining side before closing.

7. Cut two small pieces of stiff paper to fit top portion of cola cans and two to fit yellow areas of chips bags. Using permanent marker, print "COLA" and "CHIPS" on corresponding paper. Glue paper to fronts of stitched pieces.

8. Using photo as a guide and with wrong sides facing, glue cupcakes, cola cans and chips together, placing ribbon between pieces.

9. Attach fishing line through holes indicated at top of basket with a Lark's Head Knot. Tie ends together in a knot to form a loop for hanging.

Picnic Chips Bag
5 holes x 8 holes
Cut 2

Picnic Cola Can
3 holes x 5 holes
Cut 2

Picnic Cupcake
6 holes x 6 holes
Cut 2

Crawly Critters

Delight the critter lover in your family with creepy crawlies
that are more cute than scary. DESIGN BY PATRICIA KLESH

Skill Level
Beginner

Size
21 inches L x 3⅛ inches in
diameter (53.3cm x 8cm)
when hanging

Materials
- 1 sheet 7-count
  plastic canvas
- Worsted weight yarn as
  listed in color key
- 6-strand embroidery as
  listed in color key
- #16 tapestry needle
- 2 (16-inch/40.6cm) lengths
  ⅛-inch/3mm-wide green
  satin ribbon
- 7 (10-inch/5.4cm) lengths
  ¼-inch/7mm-wide green
  satin ribbon
- 7 (10-inch/5.4cm) lengths
  ¼-inch/7mm-wide satin
  ribbon in assorted colors
- 1-inch (2.5cm) white
  plastic ring
- Hot-glue gun

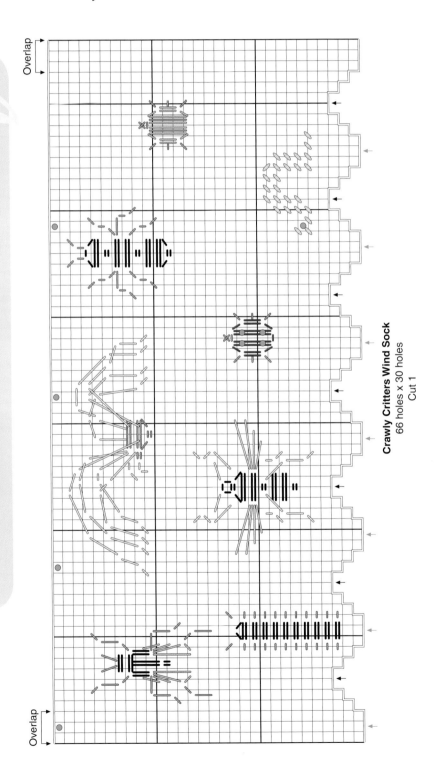

Crawly Critters Wind Sock
66 holes x 30 holes
Cut 1

Instructions

1. Cut wind sock from plastic canvas according to graph.

2. Overlap three holes indicated, then work overlapped area with white Continental Stitches. Work worsted weight yarn stitches for bugs' bodies and wings before filling in remaining background with white Continental Stitches.

3. When background stitching is completed, work legs, antennae and eyes with 6-strand embroidery floss.

4. For hanger, fold both lengths of ⅛-inch/3mm-wide green ribbon in half. Attach folded ends to white plastic ring with a Lark's Head Knot.

5. Make sure lengths are even, trimming ends if necessary. Thread ends from front to back through holes indicated on graph, keeping threaded lengths even. Glue ends to wrong side.

6. Center and glue lengths of ¼-inch/7mm-wide green ribbon to wrong side of wind sock at lowest points of scalloped edges (green arrows).

7. Center and glue lengths of assorted colors of ribbon to wrong side at highest points of scalloped edges (black arrows). ✎

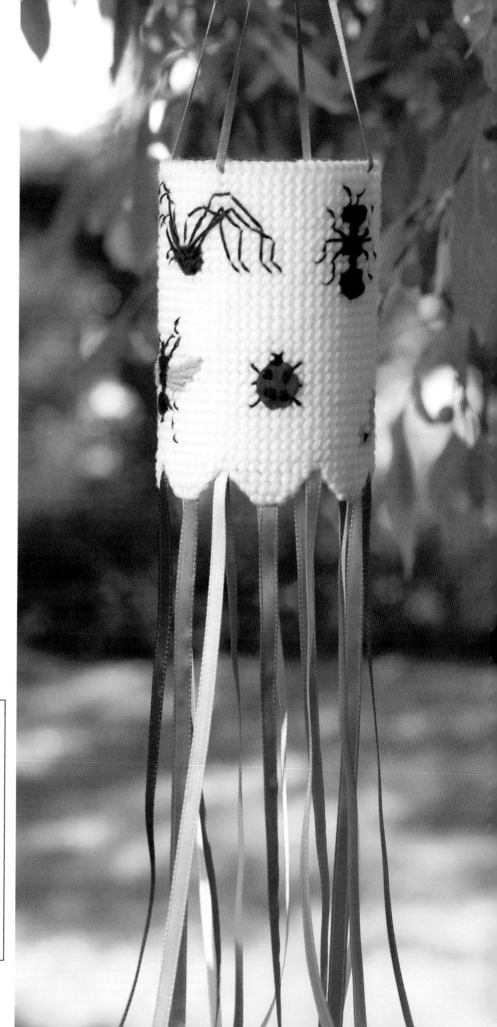

COLOR KEY		
Yards	**Worsted Weight Yarn**	
1 (1m)	☐ Bright green	
35 (32m)	Uncoded background is white Continental Stitches	
	⁄ White Overcasting	
2 (1.9m)	✏ Black Straight Stitch	
1 (1m)	✏ Red Backstitch and Straight Stitch	
1 (1m)	⁄ Light clay Straight Stitch	
1 (1m)	⁄ Gray Straight Stitch	
1 (1m)	⁄ Orange Straight Stitch	
1 (1m)	⁄ Brown Straight Stitch	
	6-Strand Embroidery Floss	
3 (2.8m)	⁄ Black Backstitch and Straight Stitch	
1 (1.9m)	⁄ Brown Backstitch	
	● Black French Knot	
	● Attach ribbon hanger	

A Howdy Welcome

Welcome your cowboys home from the roundup with a Western boot that jingles its own tune. DESIGN BY PATRICIA KLESH

Skill Level
Beginner

Size
4¾ inches W x 14¾ inches L (12.1cm x 37.5cm) when hanging

Materials
- ½ sheet 7-count plastic canvas
- Worsted weight yarn as listed in color key
- #16 tapestry needle
- 5 (2¾–3⅛-inch/7–8cm) long 6mm silver wind chimes
- 10 inches (25.4cm) gray leather lace
- Clear thread or fishing line
- Hot-glue gun

Instructions
1. Cut boots from plastic canvas according to graph.
2. Stitch one boot following graph. Reverse remaining boot before stitching.
3. String chimes on desired lengths of clear thread or fishing line. Stitch or glue to wrong side of one boot at instep, keeping edges of boot free of glue.
4. For hanger, glue ends of leather lace to wrong side of boot where indicated at arrows, keeping edges free of glue.
5. Whipstitch wrong sides of boot together, working around clear thread or fishing line at bottom and leather lace at top. ✗

COLOR KEY	
Yards	**Worsted Weight Yarn**
4 (3.7m)	☐ Dark gray
3 (2.8m)	☐ Turquoise
3 (2.8m)	☐ White
19 (17.4m)	Uncoded areas are black Continental Stitches
	✗ Black Whipstitching

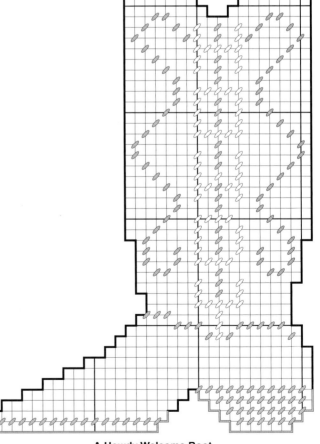

A Howdy Welcome Boot
31 holes x 42 holes
Cut 2, reverse 1

Tulip Wind Sock

Pretty both indoors and out, this project features ribbon streamers that will dance in the breeze. DESIGN BY PATRICIA KLESH

Skill Level

Beginner

Size

3¾ inches W x 16 inches L (9.5cm x 40.6cm) when hanging

Materials

- ½ sheet 7-count plastic canvas
- Worsted weight yarn as listed in color key
- #16 tapestry needle
- 6 (9-inch/22.9cm) lengths ¼-inch/7mm-wide green satin ribbon
- 2 (16-inch/40.6cm) lengths ⅛-inch/3mm-wide white satin ribbon
- 1-inch (2.5cm) white plastic ring
- Hot-glue gun

Instructions

1. Cut six tulips and one band from plastic canvas according to graphs.

2. Stitch and Overcast one tulip with pink as graphed and one each with purple, yellow, red, blue and orange.

3. Stitch band following graph, overlapping two holes of side edges before stitching. Overcast top and bottom edges.

4. Glue one green ribbon behind each tulip, placing end at sixth bar from bottom edge. Glue tulips evenly spaced around outside of band.

5. Holding both lengths of white ribbon together, fold in half. Attach folded end to white plastic ring with a Lark's Head Knot. Glue four ends evenly spaced to inside of band.

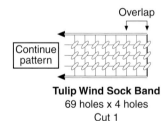

Tulip Wind Sock Band
69 holes x 4 holes
Cut 1

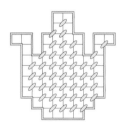

Wind Sock Tulip
10 holes x 10 holes
Cut 6
Stitch 1 as graphed
and 1 each with
purple, yellow, red,
blue and orange

COLOR KEY	
Yards	**Worsted Weight Yarn**
5 (4.6m)	☐ White
2 (1.9m)	☐ Pink
2 (1.9m)	Purple
2 (1.9m)	Yellow
2 (1.9m)	Red
2 (1.9m)	Blue
2 (1.9m)	Orange

Stars & Hearts Wind Chime

Enjoy a warm evening with the delicate jingle from this patriotic wind chime. You'll enjoy this piece year-round! DESIGN BY ANGIE ARICKX

Skill Level
Beginner

Size
5⅜ inches W x 13½ inches L (13.7cm x 34.3cm) when hanging

Materials
- 2 (5-inch) Uniek QuickShape plastic canvas stars
- Coats & Clark Red Heart Super Saver worsted weight yarn Art. E300 as listed in color key
- #16 tapestry needle
- 12 inches (30.5cm) Uniek Needloft white #55043 solid craft cord
- 4 (2¾–4 inches/7–10.2cm) wind chimes
- 24 inches (61cm) 12-pound nylon fishing line

Instructions

1. Stitch stars following graph. Whipstitch wrong sides together with white.

2. Cut four 6-inch (15.2cm) lengths fishing line. Thread lengths through stars where indicated on graph with green dots and through chimes; knot fishing line.

3. For hanger, thread white craft cord through hole indicated by yellow dot at top of assembled star. Tie ends together in a knot at desired length to form a loop for hanging. Trim ends as needed. ✄

COLOR KEY	
Yards	**Worsted Weight Yarn**
12 (11m)	☐ White #311
6 (5.5m)	■ Burgundy #376
5 (4.6m)	■ Soft navy #387
	● Attach wind chime
	○ Attach hanger cord

Color numbers given are for Coats & Clark Red Heart Super Saver worsted weight yarn Art. E300.

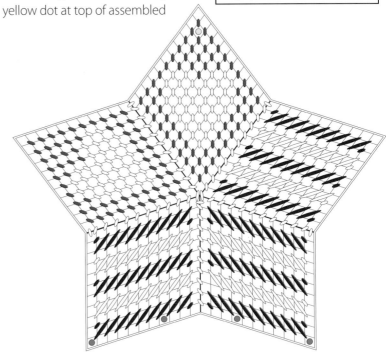

Stars & Hearts Wind Chime Star
Stitch 2

Table Decor

Decorate your porch or patio table for any occasion with a variety of pieces suitable for casual outdoor dining.

Super Burger Coasters

Super-size your next meal with coasters loaded with all the extras. DESIGNS BY RONDA BRYCE

Skill Level

Beginner

Size

Stacked Super Burger: $5\frac{1}{2}$ inches H x $5\frac{5}{8}$ inches in diameter (14cm x 14.3cm)
Bun Top: 3 inches W x $1\frac{3}{4}$ H (7.6cm x 4.4cm), excluding flag
Plate with Bun Bottom and Chips: $1\frac{1}{4}$ H x $5\frac{5}{8}$ inches in diameter (3.2cm x 14.3cm)
Hamburgers: $3\frac{3}{4}$ inches in diameter (9.5cm)
Onion: $3\frac{3}{4}$ inches in diameter (9.5cm)
American Cheese: $3\frac{1}{2}$ inches W x $3\frac{1}{4}$ H (8.9cm x 8.3cm)
Swiss Cheese: $3\frac{1}{2}$ inches W x $3\frac{1}{4}$ H (8.9cm x 8.3cm)
Tomato: $3\frac{1}{2}$ inches W x $3\frac{1}{4}$ H (8.9cm x 8.3cm)
Lettuce: $4\frac{1}{4}$ inches square (10.8cm), including rickrack
Pickles with Mayo: $3\frac{1}{2}$ inches W x $3\frac{1}{4}$ H (8.9cm x 8.3cm)

Materials

- 1 sheet 7-count plastic
- 1 (6-inch) Uniek QuickShape plastic canvas radial circle
- 3 (4-inch) Uniek QuickShape plastic canvas radial circles
- 2 (3-inch) Uniek QuickShape plastic canvas radial circles
- 1 (3-inch) Uniek QuickShape plastic canvas 3-D globe
- Uniek Needloft plastic canvas yarn as listed in color key
- Coats & Clark Red Heart Super Saver worsted weight yarn Art. E300 as listed in color key
- #16 tapestry needle
- 1 yard (1m) emerald jumbo rickrack
- 60 black glass seed beads
- $2\frac{1}{2}$-inch flag pick
- Hand-sewing needle
- Beige and green sewing thread

Bun Top

1. Cut connecting tabs from one half of globe. Stitch and Overcast piece (page 145) with worsted weight yarn following graph.
2. Using hand-sewing needle and beige thread, attach beads for sesame seeds as desired.
3. Insert flag pick through hole in top.

Plate, Bun Bottom & Chips

1. Cut chips and bun bottom side from plastic canvas according to graphs (pages 144 and 145).
2. Using plastic canvas yarn throughout, stitch and Overcast plate (page 145), leaving area indicated inside red line unstitched. Stitch and Overcast chips following graph, using double strand eggshell.
3. Stitch bun bottom top (page 145) and side with worsted weight yarn following graphs. Using buff, Whipstitch short edges of side together, then Whipstitch side to top. Overcast bottom edges.
4. Using hand-sewing needle and beige thread throughout, tack bun bottom over unstitched area of plate, placing bun a little off center (see photo). Tack chips to bun and plate.

Hamburger & Onion

1. Cut two outermost rows of holes (gray area) from hamburgers and onion (pages 144 and 145).
2. Stitch and Overcast pieces with plastic canvas yarn following graphs.

Cheese Slices

1. Cut Swiss cheese slice from plastic canvas according to graph (page 144), cutting out eight holes. Cut one 23-hole x 21-hole piece for American cheese slice.
2. Using plastic canvas yarn throughout, stitch and Overcast inside and outside edges of Swiss cheese slice following graph. Continental Stitch and

Overcast American cheese slice with tangerine.

Tomato & Lettuce
1. Cut pieces from plastic canvas according to graphs (page 144).
2. Using plastic canvas yarn throughout, Continental Stitch and Overcast lettuce with Christmas green. Stitch and Overcast tomato following graph, working uncoded areas with Christmas red Continental Stitches.

3. When background stitching is completed, work lemon Straight Stitches on tomato.
4. Using hand-sewing needle and green thread, sew rickrack to back side of lettuce around outer edges, overlapping ends and trimming to fit.

Pickles & Mayo
1. Cut piece from plastic canvas according to graph (page 144).
2. Stitch and Overcast with

plastic canvas yarn following graph, working uncoded areas with Christmas green Continental Stitches.
3. When background stitching is completed, work lemon Straight Stitches where indicated.

Finishing
1. When coasters are not in use, stack pieces as desired on bun bottom, placing bun top on top of stack. 🦋

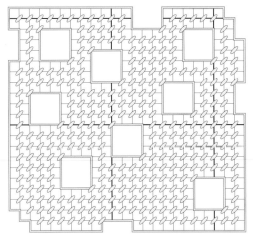

Super Burger Swiss Cheese Slice
23 holes x 21 holes
Cut 1
Stitch with plastic canvas yarn

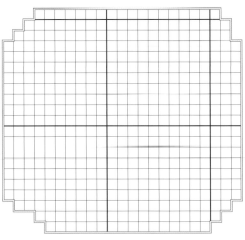

Super Burger Lettuce
23 holes x 21 holes
Cut 1
Stitch with plastic canvas yarn

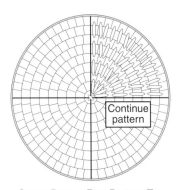

Super Burger Bun Bottom Top
Stitch 1 (3-inch) radial circle
with worsted weight yarn

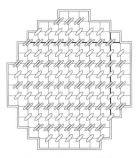

Super Burger Chip
12 holes x 13 holes
Cut 2
Stitch with plastic canvas yarn

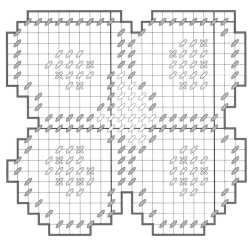

Super Burger Pickles With Mayo
23 holes x 21 holes
Cut 1
Stitch with plastic canvas yarn

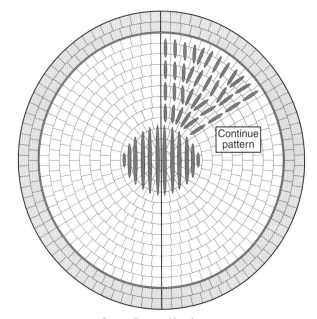

Continue
pattern

Super Burger Hamburger
Cut 2 from 4-inch radial circles,
cutting away gray area
Stitch with plastic canvas yarn

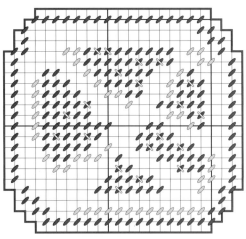

Super Burger Tomato
23 holes x 21 holes
Cut 1
Stitch with plastic canvas yarn

COLOR KEY

Yards	Plastic Canvas Yarn
7 (6.5m)	■ Red #01
10 (9.2m)	Tangerine #11
15 (13.8m)	■ Cinnamon #14
7 (6.5m)	□ Lemon #20
3 (2.8m)	□ Fern #23
3 (2.8m)	■ Holly #27
13 (11.9m)	■ Royal #32
23 (21.1m)	□ Eggshell #39
7 (6.5m)	□ White #41
2 (1.9m)	■ Watermelon #55
5 (4.6m)	Uncoded areas on tomato are Christmas red #02 Continental Stitches
13 (11.9m)	Uncoded areas on pickle and lettuce are Christmas green #28 Continental Stitches
	⁄ Lemon #20 Straight Stitch
	⁄ Christmas green #28 Overcasting
3 (2.8m)	⁄ Forest #29 Overcasting
	Worsted Weight Yarn
8 (7.4m)	□ Aran #313
8 (7.4m)	□ Buff #334
3 (2.8m)	■ Warm brown #336

Color numbers given are for Uniek Needloft plastic canvas yarn and Coats & Clark Red Heart Super Saver worsted weight yarn Art. E300.

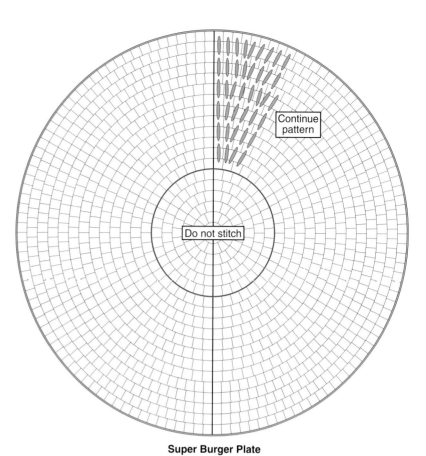

Super Burger Plate
Stitch 1 (6-inch) radial circle
with plastic canvas yarn
Do not stitch area
inside red circle

Super Burger Bun Bottom Side
62 holes x 3 holes
Cut 1
Stitch with worsted weight yarn

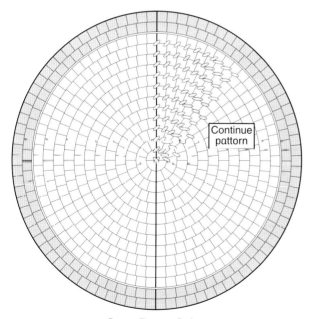

Super Burger Onion
Cut 1 from 4-inch radial circle,
cutting away gray area
Stitch with plastic canvas yarn

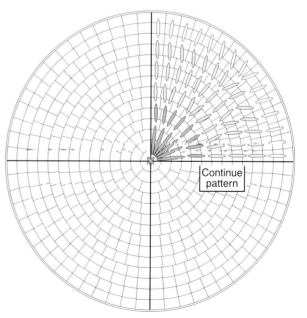

Super Burger Bun Top
Cut connecting tabs off
1 portion of globe
Stitch with worsted weight yarn

Rain Forest Coaster Set

Ready to take flight, this butterfly coaster set is so realistic you can almost hear the sounds of the rain forest. DESIGNS BY TERRY RICIOLI

Skill Level
Beginner

Size
Coasters: 5⅝ inches W x 4⅞ inches H (14.3cm x 12.4cm)

Coaster Holder: 5 inches W x 3⅞ inches H x 1⅝ inches D (12.7cm x 9.8cm x 4.1cm)

Materials
- 1 sheet clear 7-count plastic canvas
- ¼ sheet green 7-count plastic canvas
- Uniek Needloft plastic canvas yarn as listed in color key
- 2 sheets self-adhesive black felt (optional)

Instructions

1. Cut four butterfly coasters and two leaf shapes for holder front and back from clear plastic canvas according to graphs (this page and pages 148 and 149).

2. Cut one base from green plastic canvas according to graph (page 149). Also from green plastic canvas, cut one 10-hole x 10-hole piece for large side and one 10-hole x 2-hole piece for small side. Base and sides will remain unstitched.

3. Stitch and Overcast butterfly coasters following graphs, working uncoded areas on right side of bodies and wings with black Continental Stitches and uncoded areas on left side of bodies and wings with black Reverse Continental Stitches.

4. Stitch one holder leaf following graph. Reverse remaining leaf and work stitching in reverse. When background stitching is complete, work moss Backstitches for leaf veins.

5. Using Christmas green throughout, Whipstitch bottom edges of leaves to base piece where indicated on graphs. Whipstitch large side to leaves where indicated,

Rain Forest Butterfly Coaster A
37 holes x 32 holes
Cut 1 from clear

then Whipstitch small side to leaves and base where indicated. Overcast remaining edges of leaves.

5. If desired, cut felt to fit butterflies and adhere to wrong sides. 🌿

COLOR KEY

Yards	Plastic Canvas Yarn
4 (3.7m)	☐ Tangerine #11 (butterfly A)
3 (2.8m)	☐ Pumpkin #12 (butterflies A and D)
3 (2.8m)	☐ Fern #23 (butterfly B)
4 (3.7m)	☐ Moss #25 (holder leaf)
12 (11m)	■ Christmas green #28 (holder leaf)
2 (1.9m)	☐ Mermaid #53 (butterfly C)
4 (3.7m)	■ Watermelon #55 (butterfly D)
2 (1.9m)	☐ Yellow #57 (butterfly B)
3 (2.8m)	☐ Bright blue #60 (butterfly C)
2 (1.9m)	☐ Bright purple #64 (butterfly A)
18 (16.5m)	Uncoded areas on right side of bodies and wings are black #00 Continental Stitches
	Uncoded areas on left side of bodies and wings are black #00 Reverse Continental Stitches
	✏ Black #00 Overcasting
	✏ Moss #25 Backstitch

Color numbers given are for Uniek Needloft plastic canvas yarn.

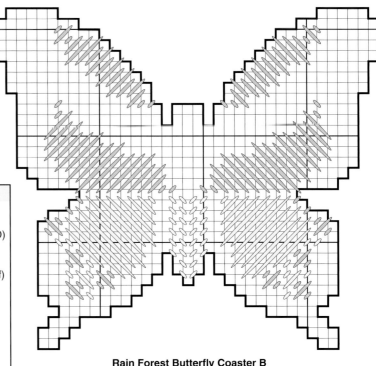

Rain Forest Butterfly Coaster B
37 holes x 32 holes
Cut 1 from clear

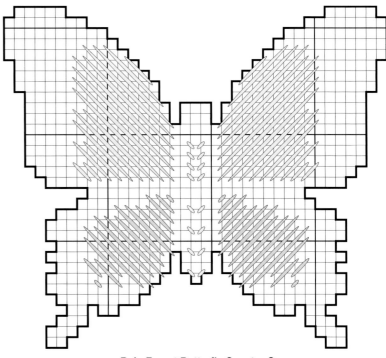

Rain Forest Butterfly Coaster C
37 holes x 32 holes
Cut 1 from clear

Rain Forest Butterfly Coaster D
37 holes x 32 holes
Cut 1 from clear

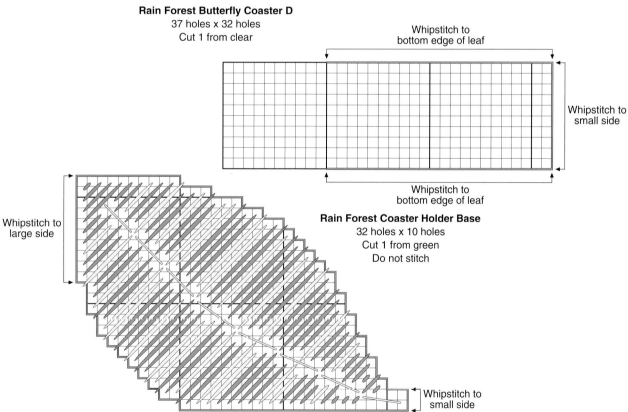

Whipstitch to
bottom edge of leaf

Whipstitch to
small side

Whipstitch to
bottom edge of leaf

Rain Forest Coaster Holder Base
32 holes x 10 holes
Cut 1 from green
Do not stitch

Whipstitch to
large side

Whipstitch to
small side

Whipstitch
to base

**Rain Forest Coaster Holder
Leaf Front & Back**
32 holes x 22 holes
Cut 2 from clear
Stitch 1 as graphed
Reverse 1 and work
stitches in reverse

Lemonade Straw Keeper

Sip your favorite beverage while stitching this 1950s-inspired beverage accessory. DESIGN BY GINA WOODS

Skill Level
Beginner

Size
3¼ inches H x 9 inches H x 3¼ D (8.3cm x 22.9cm x 8.3cm)

Materials
- 1¼ sheets clear stiff 7-count plastic canvas
- ¼ sheet yellow 7-count plastic canvas
- Worsted weight yarn as listed in color key
- Metallic craft cord as listed in color key
- 6-strand embroidery floss as listed in color key
- #16 tapestry needle
- Hot-glue gun

Instructions
1. Cut front, back, sides and top from clear stiff plastic canvas according to graphs (pages 151 and 152). Cut one 20-hole x 20-hole piece from yellow plastic canvas for base. Base will remain unstitched.
2. Stitch and Overcast leaves, working Straight Stitch when Background stitching is completed.
3. Stitch remaining pieces

following graphs, working uncoded areas with white background in dark blue Continental Stitches and uncoded areas with yellow background in pale yellow Continental Stitches.

4. When background stitching is complete, use yarn to work lime green Lazy Daisy Stitches, bright yellow French Knots, wrapping yarn two times, and red Straight Stitches to stripe letters.

5. Using floss, work light blue Backstitches to complete lettering and white Straight Stitches for lemon sections.

6. For striped straws and striped Straight Stitches on top, thread needle with both red and white yarn. Come up in one hole of Straight Stitch, twist yarn until colors are spiraled, then go down in ending hole of Straight Stitch.

7. Overcast inside edges on front with pale yellow. Using dark blue, Whipstitch front and back to sides, then Whipstitch front, back and sides to top and to unstitched base.

8. Glue leaves to top left rim of glass where indicated on graph.

9. Insert and remove straws through opening in front. 🌿

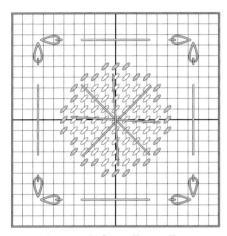

Lemonade Straw Keeper Top
20 holes x 20 holes
Cut 1 from clear stiff

COLOR KEY

Yards	Worsted Weight Yarn
24 (22m)	☐ White
22 (20.2m)	■ Red
16 (14.7m)	☐ Bright yellow
5 (4.6m)	▨ Lime green
3 (2.8m)	▨ Honey gold
2 (1.9m)	☐ Powder blue
75 (68.6m)	Uncoded areas with white background are dark blue Continental Stitches
22 (20.2m)	Uncoded areas with yellow background are pale yellow Continental Stitches
	∕ Dark blue Whipstitching
	∕ Pale yellow Overcasting
	⟋ Red Straight Stitch
	∕ Lime green Straight Stitch
	∕ Combined and twisted red and white Straight Stitch
	⌀ Lime green Lazy Daisy Stitch
	○ Bright yellow (2-wrap) French Knot
4 (3.7m)	**Metallic Craft Cord**
	▨ Iridescent white
5 (4.6m)	**6-Strand Embroidery Floss**
2 (1.9m)	∕ Light blue Backstitch
	∕ White Straight Stitch
	● Attach leaves

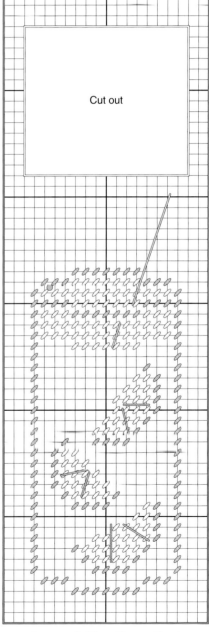

Lemonade Straw Keeper Front
20 holes x 59 holes
Cut 1 from clear stiff

**Lemonade Straw Keeper
Small Leaf**
5 holes x 5 holes
Cut 1 from clear stiff

**Lemonade Straw Keeper
Large Leaf**
7 holes x 7 holes
Cut 1 from clear stiff

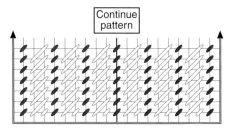

Lemonade Straw Keeper Back
20 holes x 59 holes
Cut 1 from clear stiff

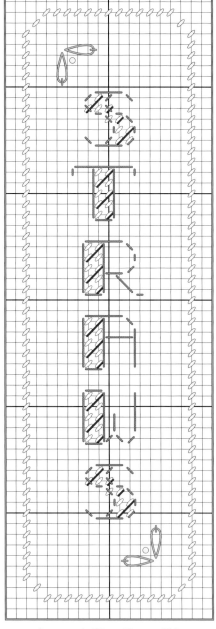

Lemonade Straw Keeper Side
20 holes x 59 holes
Cut 2 from clear stiff

Daisy Picnic Set

Entertain in style at your next soiree with a coordinating coaster and place-mat set emblazoned with cheerful daisies. DESIGNS BY ALIDA MACOR

Skill Level

Beginner

Size

Place Mat: 13⅝ inches W x 10⅝ inches H (34.6cm x 27cm)
Coasters: 3⅞ inches W x 3⅞ inches H (9.8cm x 9.8cm)

Materials

Place Mat & Coasters
- Worsted weight yarn as listed in color key
- #16 tapestry needle

Place Mat
- 1 sheet pastel blue 7-count plastic canvas
- 1¼ sheets white 7-count plastic canvas

Coasters
- 1 sheet pastel blue 7-count plastic canvas
- ½ sheet white 7-count plastic canvas

Place Mat

1. Cut place mat top from pastel blue plastic canvas according to graph.

2. Set aside one full sheet white plastic canvas for place mat base. Cut four daisies from remaining white plastic canvas according to graph.

3. Place daisies in corners of place mat top where indicated with red lines. Following daisy graph, work white and light orange stitches through both layers. Work chartreuse stitches for leaves.

4. Place top over base, then Whipstitch together around outside edges. Whipstitch inner edges of top to base with light blue Straight Stitches, using one stitch per hole along top, bottom and side edges; use two stitches per hole at corners.

Coasters

1. Cut coaster base pieces from pastel blue plastic canvas and daisies from white plastic canvas according to graphs.

2. Place one daisy on each base where indicated with red lines. Following daisy graph, work white and light orange stitches through both layers. Work chartreuse stitches for leaves.

3. Overcast around outside edges of base pieces with light blue. 🌿

**Daisy Picnic Set
Place Mat Daisy**
11 holes x 11 holes
Cut 4 from white

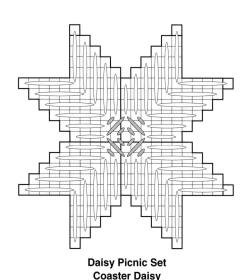

**Daisy Picnic Set
Coaster Daisy**
21 holes x 21 holes
Cut 6 from white

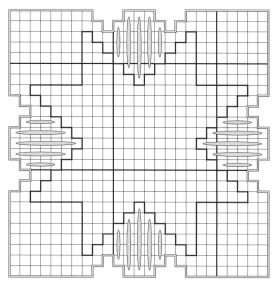

Daisy Picnic Set Coaster Base
25 holes x 25 holes
Cut 6 from pastel blue

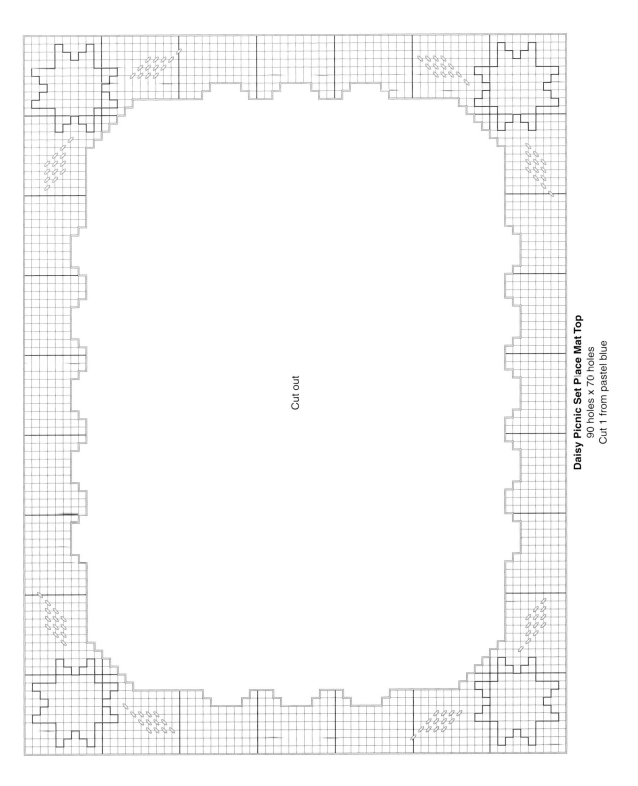

Cut out

Daisy Picnic Set Place Mat Top
90 holes x 70 holes
Cut 1 from pastel blue

Can & Bottle Cozies

Stitch up several of these for your next outdoor party. Ideal for holding cans or bottles, they're sure to help your guests keep their drinks identified. DESIGNS BY GINA WOODS

Skill Level
Beginner

Size
3⁹⁄₁₆ inches H x 3½ inches in diameter (9.1cm x 8.9cm)

Materials
- 2⅓ sheets 7-count plastic canvas
- 7 (3-inch) Darice plastic canvas radial circles
- Worsted weight yarn as listed in color key
- 6-strand embroidery floss as listed in color key
- #16 tapestry needle

Project Note
The diamond, flower, heart, star, square, triangle and inverted triangle symbols used on graphs all designate Continental Stitches.

Instructions
1. Cut plastic canvas according to graphs (pages 158, 159 and 160). Do not cut plastic canvas radial circles which will be bases for cozies.
2. Stitch sides following graphs, overlapping three holes on side edges before stitching and working uncoded background with Continental Stitches as follows: American flag with navy blue, cherries with pink, flower with dark green, heart with lilac, rainbow with light blue, shamrock with bright green, watermelon with medium yellow.
3. When background stitching is completed, work black yarn Straight Stitches for seeds on watermelon cozy and white floss French Knots for stars on American flag cozy.

4. Stitch one base piece with light blue as graphed and one each with navy blue, pink, dark green, lilac, bright green and medium yellow.
5. Using matching colors, Whipstitch sides to matching base pieces; Overcast top edges. ❧

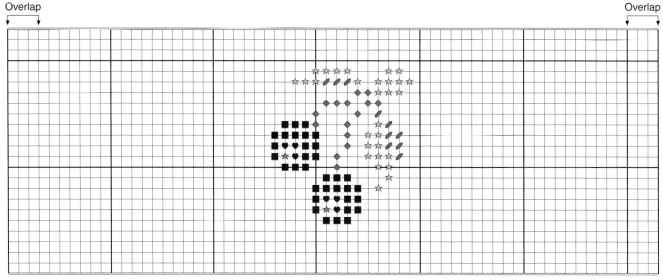

Cherries Cozy
63 holes x 23 holes
Cut 1

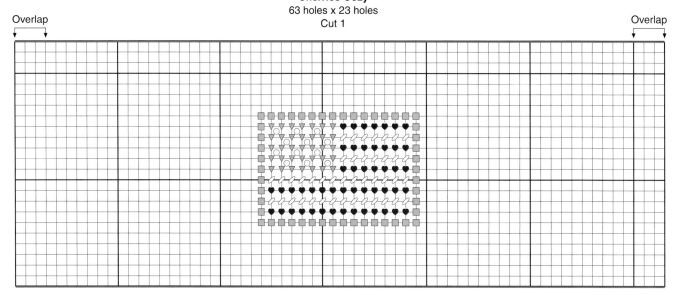

American Flag Cozy
63 holes x 23 holes
Cut 1

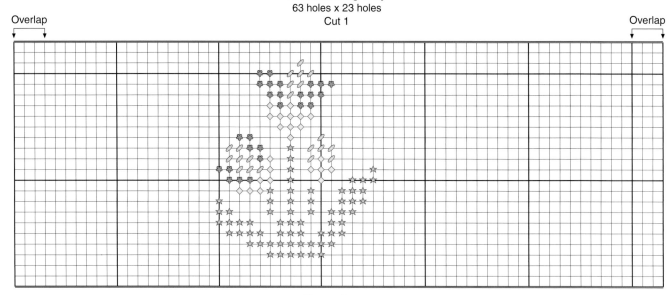

Flower Cozy
63 holes x 23 holes
Cut 1

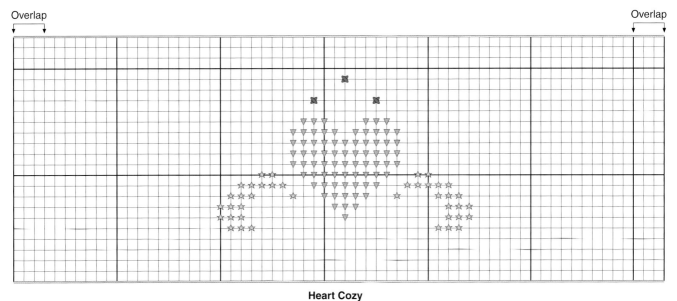

Heart Cozy
63 holes x 23 holes
Cut 1

Rainbow Cozy
63 holes x 23 holes
Cut 1

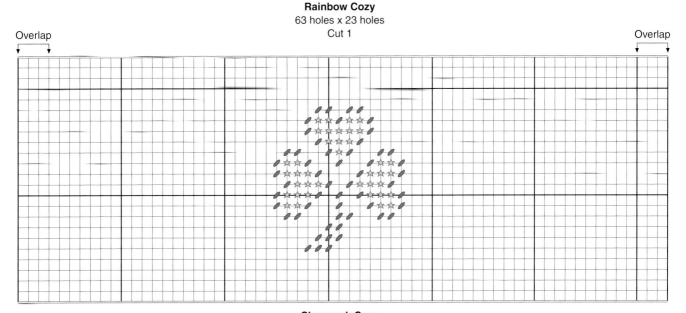

Shamrock Cozy
63 holes x 23 holes
Cut 1

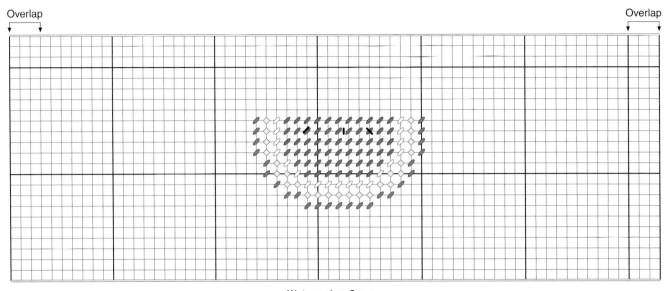

Watermelon Cozy
63 holes x 23 holes
Cut 1

COLOR KEY

Yards		Worsted Weight Yarn
26 (23.8m)	⬩	Dark green
24 (22m)	◇	Bright green
22 (20.2m)	⬩	Light blue
4 (3.7m)	☆	Medium green
4 (3.7m)	♥	Red
3 (2.8m)	▽	Medium purple
2 (1.9m)	▽	Royal blue
2 (1.9m)	⬩	White
2 (1.9m)	⬛	Gold
2 (1.9m)	⬩	Orange
2 (1.9m)	⬩	Deep pink
1 (1m)	★	Light red
1 (1m)	◼	Maroon
1 (1m)	◆	Brown
1 (1m)	✿	Red orange
1 (1m)	△	Yellow
1 (1m)	⬩	Purple
		Uncoded background on shamrock is bright green Continental Stitches
22 (20.2m)		Uncoded background on American flag is navy blue Continental Stitches
22 (20.2m)		Uncoded background on cherries is pink Continental Stitches
		Uncoded background on flower is dark green Continental Stitches
22 (20.2m)		Uncoded background on heart is lilac Continental Stitches
		Uncoded background on rainbow is light blue Continental Stitches
22 (20.2m)		Uncoded background on watermelon is medium yellow Continental Stitches
	⬩	Navy blue Overcasting and Whipstitching
	⬩	Pink Overcasting and Whipstitching
	⬩	Lilac Overcasting and Whipstitching
	⬩	Medium yellow Overcasting and Whipstitching
1 (1m)	⬩	Black Straight Stitch
		6-Strand Embroidery Floss
1 (1m)	○	White French Knot

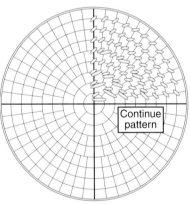

Cozy Base
Stitch 1 with light blue as graphed
Stitch 1 each with navy blue,
pink, dark green, lilac
bright green and medium yellow

Watermelon Picnic Pockets

Pick your favorite shade of plastic canvas and keep your napkin and plastic picnic-ware close at hand. DESIGN BY ALIDA MACOR

Skill Level
Beginner

Size
4¾ inches W x 9⅛ inches H
(12.1cm x 23.2cm)

Materials
One Pocket
- 1 sheet 7-count plastic canvas in desired color
- Worsted weight yarn as listed in color key
- #16 tapestry needle
- 6 (4mm) black beads
- Hand-sewing needle
- Black sewing thread

Project Note
Instructions and amounts given are for one pocket. Samples show three pockets, using yellow, pastel pink and white plastic canvas.

Instructions
1. Cut one back and one front from plastic canvas according to graphs (this page and page 162).
2. Stitch front following graph, working Slanted Gobelin Stitches at top in yarn color to match plastic canvas. Pocket back will remain unstitched.
3. Using hand-sewing needle and black thread, attach beads where indicated on graph.
4. Place front on back, matching bottom and side edges. Using 1¼ yards (1.2m) yarn that matches plastic canvas, Whipstitch front to back in every other hole, beginning and ending at top corners of pocket front. 🌿

COLOR KEY	
Yards	**Worsted Weight Yarn**
7 (6.5m)	▨ Hot pink
3 (2.8m)	☐ Color to match plastic canvas
2 (1.9m)	☐ White
2 (1.9m)	▨ Green
	● Attach bead

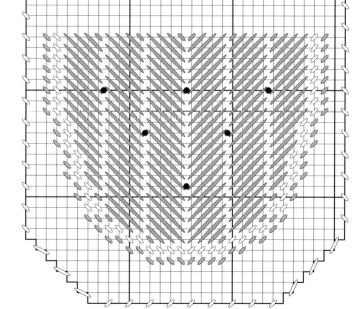

Watermelon Picnic Pocket Front
31 holes x 31 holes
Cut 1

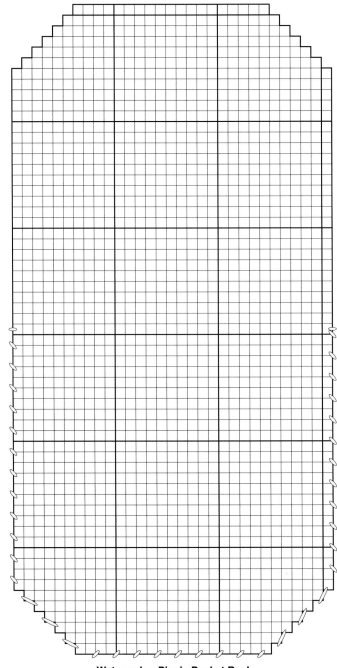

Watermelon Picnic Pocket Back
31 holes x 61 holes
Cut 1

Teatime Napkin Holder

This delightful holder is embellished with fanciful flowers and will keep napkins close at hand. DESIGN BY ALIDA MACOR

Skill Level
Beginner

Size
9½ inches W x 6½ inches H x 1¾ D (24.1cm x 16.5cm x 4.4cm)

Materials
- 2½ sheets white 7-count plastic canvas
- Worsted weight yarn as listed in color key
- DMC #3 pearl cotton as listed in color key
- #16 tapestry needle

Instructions

1. Cut four holder front and back pieces according to graph. Cut four 10-hole x 10-hole pieces for holder sides and two 46-hole x 10-hole pieces for holder base. Side and base pieces will remain unstitched.

2. Stitch one front piece following graph, working uncoded areas on white background with white

Continental Stitches. Do not stitch uncoded areas with pale blue background. Reverse one back piece and work design following graph, using center bar of graph as reference.

3. When background stitching is completed, work very dark blue green pearl cotton Backstitches.

4. Using 3 yards (2.8m) light green yarn, Whipstitch unstitched front to stitched front, beginning at top and working half yarn in each direction to light green dots. Using white, Whipstitch inside edges together.

5. Repeat Step 4 for stitched and unstitched back pieces.

6. Using white, Whipstitch two side pieces together along top edges. Using same length of yarn, Whipstitch sides to front where indicated, working through all four layers.

7. Repeat step 6 for other side of front, then Whipstitch sides to back, again working through all four layers.

8. Place two base pieces together, then Whipstitch to front, back and sides, working through all layers. 🍂

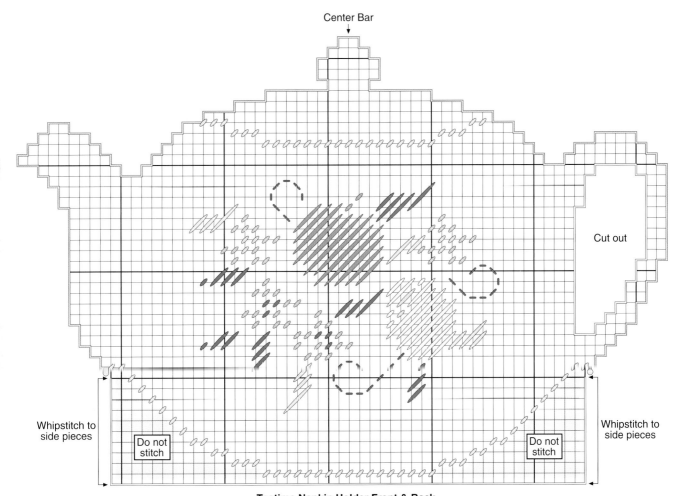

Center Bar

Cut out

Whipstitch to side pieces

Do not stitch

Do not stitch

Whipstitch to side pieces

Teatime Napkin Holder Front & Back
63 holes x 42 holes
Cut 4
Stitch 1 as graphed
Reverse 1 before stitching
2 will remain unstitched

Lighthouse Frame

Frame your favorite summer vacation photo in this nautical-themed project. DESIGN BY RUBY THACKER

Skill Level
Beginner

Size
10½ inches W x 8⅜ inches H
(26.7cm x 21.3cm)

Materials
- 2 sheets 7-count plastic canvas
- Uniek Needloft plastic canvas yarn as listed in color key
- ⅛-inch/3mm-wide metallic ribbon as listed in color key
- #16 tapestry needle
- 1¼ yards (1.1m) ¼-inch (7mm) white cord trim
- Hot-glue gun

Instructions

1. Cut plastic canvas according to graphs (this page and page 168), cutting out opening on frame front only. Frame back and stand will remain unstitched.

2. Stitch and Overcast sailboat, lighthouse and stars following graphs, then work camel Straight Stitch on sailboat mast. Stitch frame front, leaving area indicated around border unworked.

3. Aligning bottom edges and using dark royal, Whipstitch long straight edge of stand to back where indicated at arrow. Overcast opening on front with gold ribbon. Using dark royal, Overcast bottom edge of front from dot to dot, then Whipstitch front to back along remaining edges.

4. Find center point of cord and begin gluing at center bottom of frame front. Glue around unworked border area, ending at center top. Tie ends together in a knot. Tie a knot in each end approximately ½–¾ inch (1.3–1.9cm) from top center knot. Trim excess cord.

5. Using photo as a guide, glue sailboat, lighthouse and stars to frame front.

6. Insert photo in frame through opening at bottom. 🌿

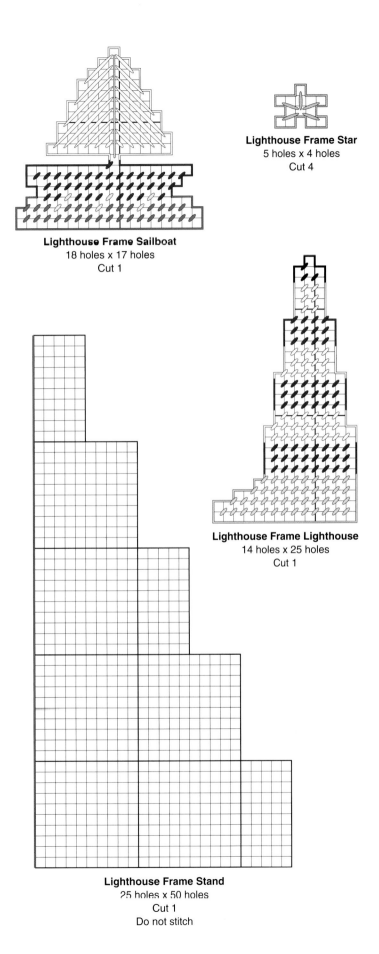

Lighthouse Frame Sailboat
18 holes x 17 holes
Cut 1

Lighthouse Frame Star
5 holes x 4 holes
Cut 4

Lighthouse Frame Lighthouse
14 holes x 25 holes
Cut 1

Lighthouse Frame Stand
25 holes x 50 holes
Cut 1
Do not stitch

COLOR KEY	
Yards	**Plastic Canvas Yarn**
1 (1m)	■ Black #00
3 (2.8m)	■ Red #01
1 (1m)	☐ Sail blue #35
3 (2.8m)	☐ White #41
2 (1.9m)	☐ Camel #43
31 (28.4m)	■ Dark royal #48
1 (1m)	☐ Yellow #57
	✏ Camel #43 Straight Stitch
	⅛-Inch-Wide Metallic Ribbon
3 (2.8m)	▨ Gold

Color numbers given are for Uniek Needloft plastic canvas yarn.

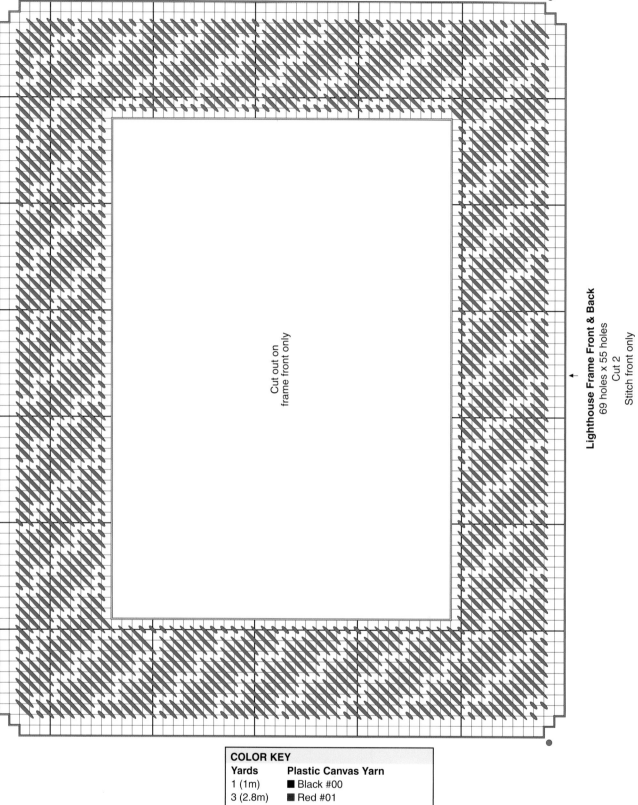

Cut out on
frame front only

Lighthouse Frame Front & Back
69 holes x 55 holes
Cut 2
Stitch front only

COLOR KEY	
Yards	**Plastic Canvas Yarn**
1 (1m)	■ Black #00
3 (2.8m)	■ Red #01
1 (1m)	□ Sail blue #35
3 (2.8m)	□ White #41
2 (1.9m)	□ Camel #43
31 (28.4m)	■ Dark royal #48
1 (1m)	□ Yellow #57
	╱ Camel #43 Straight Stitch
¹⁄₈-Inch-Wide Metallic Ribbon	
3 (2.8m)	□ Gold

Color numbers given are for Uniek Needloft
plastic canvas yarn.

Fanciful Butterflies

Enjoy the beauty of nature with a whimsical candle wrap and coordinating place mat set created in a butterfly motif. DESIGNS BY HEATHE SCHUTZE

Skill Level

Intermediate

Size

Place Mats: 14½ inches W x 10¼ inches H (36.8cm x 26cm)

Candle Wrap: Approximately 4¾ inches W x 4 inches in diameter (12.1cm x 10.2cm)

Materials

- 2 artist-size sheets 7-count plastic canvas
- 1 (80-hole x 120-hole) sheet 7-count plastic canvas
- Caron Yarn Simply Soft Brites worsted weight yarn as listed in color key
- #16 tapestry needle

Project Note

Please use caution. Plastic canvas and plastic canvas yarn will melt and burn if they get too hot or come in contact with a flame. Never leave a lighted candle unattended. Recommended for decorative purposes only.

Instructions

1. Cut place mats from artist-size plastic canvas according to graph.

2. Cut candle wrap from 80-hole x 120-hole sheet plastic canvas according to graph cutting out holes on and between butterflies.

3. Stitch and Overcast one place mat following graph. Stitch and Overcast second placemat replacing lemonade with watermelon, limelight with mango and blue mint with grape.

4. Stitch and Overcast candle wrap, overlapping five holes as indicated before stitching. 🌿

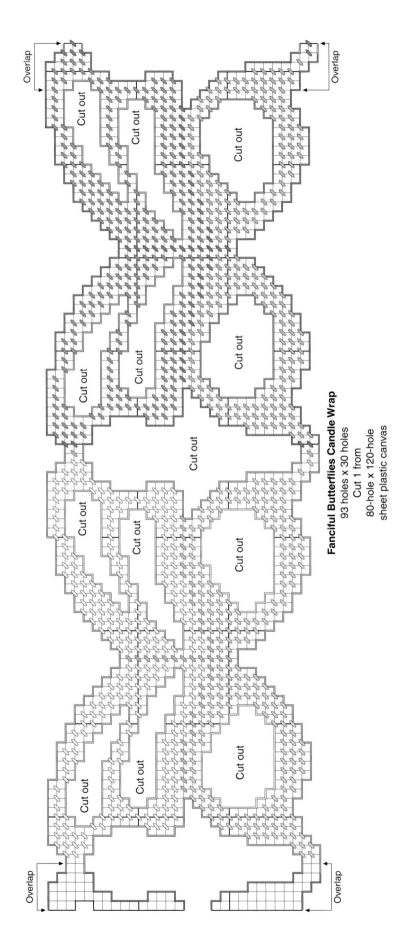

Fanciful Butterflies Candle Wrap
93 holes x 30 holes
Cut 1 from
80-hole x 120-hole
sheet plastic canvas

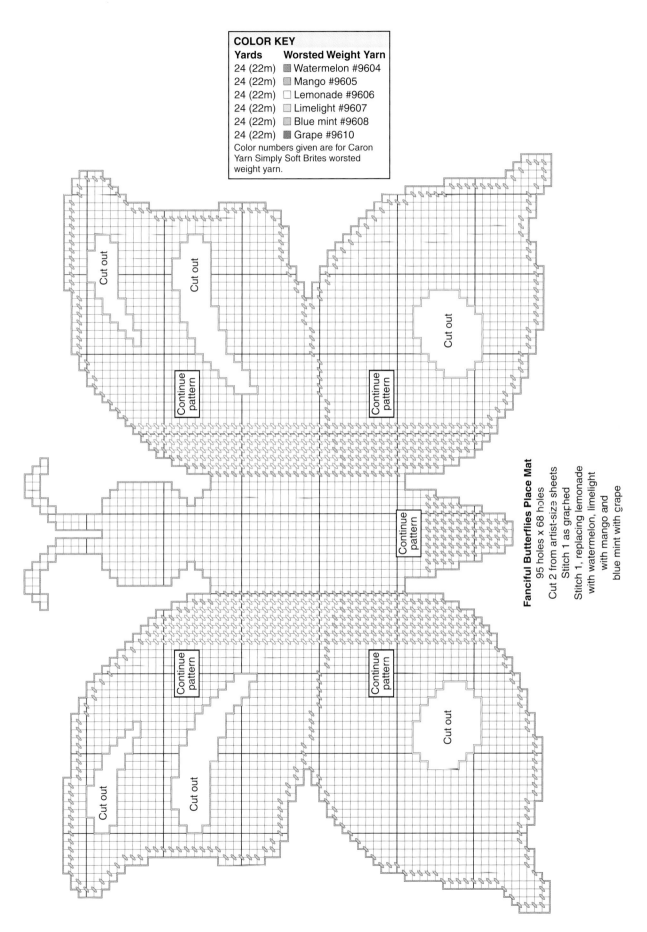

COLOR KEY

Yards	Worsted Weight Yarn
24 (22m)	Watermelon #9604
24 (22m)	Mango #9605
24 (22m)	Lemonade #9606
24 (22m)	Limelight #9607
24 (22m)	Blue mint #9608
24 (22m)	Grape #9610

Color numbers given are for Caron Yarn Simply Soft Brites worsted weight yarn.

Cut out

Cut out

Cut out

Continue pattern

Continue pattern

Continue pattern

Continue pattern

Continue pattern

Cut out

Cut out

Cut out

Fanciful Butterflies Place Mat
95 holes x 68 holes
Cut 2 from artist-size sheets
Stitch 1 as graphed
Stitch 1, replacing lemonade with watermelon, limelight with mango and blue mint with grape

Flower Votive

Add a pretty floral touch to your table with this stitched votive holder.

DESIGN BY TERRY RICIOLI

Skill Level
Beginner

Size
5⅝ inches W x 2⅛ inches H
(14.3cm x 5.4cm)

Materials
- ½ sheet 7-count plastic canvas
- Uniek Needloft plastic canvas yarn as listed in color key
- #16 tapestry needle

Project Note
Please use caution. Plastic canvas and plastic canvas yarn will melt and burn if they get too hot or come in contact with a flame. Never leave a lighted candle unattended. Recommended for decorative purposes only.

Instructions
1. Cut base and petals from plastic canvas according to graphs.
2. Stitch petals and base following graphs. Center portion of base will remain unstitched.
3. Overcast leaf portions of base only. Overcast around side and top edges of petals from dot to dot. Whipstitch dart of each petal together.
4. Whipstitch bottom edges of four inner petals to base where indicated with blue lines. Whipstitch four outer petals to base where indicated with pink lines.
5. Place glass votive holder in center of flower. 🌿

Flower Votive Petal
13 holes x 13 holes
Cut 8

Flower Votive Base
31 holes x 31 holes
Cut 1

COLOR KEY	
Yards	**Plastic Canvas Yarn**
20 (18.3m)	☐ Pink #07
20 (18.3m)	☐ Fern #23
3 (2.8m)	■ Christmas green #28
Color numbers given are for Uniek Needloft plastic canvas yarn.	

Special Thanks

We would like to acknowledge and thank the following designers whose original work has been published in this collection. We appreciate and value their creativity and dedication to designing quality plastic canvas projects!

Debra Arch
Ladybug Doorstop

Angie Arickx
Butterfly Garden
Ladybug Duo
Patriotic Swirls
Quilt Block Seedling Tray
Springtime Birdhouse
Star Pride Forever
Stars & Hearts Wind Chime

Ronda Bryce
Pot Overalls
Super Burger Coasters

Pam Bull
Birdhouse Welcome
Plant Poke Trio

Mary T. Cosgrove
Beaded Cross
Flower Boutique
Glimmer Fish
Rims & Trims

Nancy Dorman
Daisy Flyswatter
Feathered Friends Door Decor
Hot-Air Balloon Topper

Patricia Klesh
A Howdy Welcome
Basking Among the Flowers
Crawly Critters
Time for a Picnic
Tulip Wind Sock

Alida Macor
Daisy Picnic Set
He Loves Me … He Loves Me Not
Sunbonnet Cheer
Teatime Napkin Holder
Watermelon Picnic Pockets

Terry Ricioli
Flip-Flop Mobile
Floral Suncatchers
Flower Votive
Garden Angel
Nautical Doorstop
Rain Forest Coaster Set
Summer Basket

Carol Rodgers
Critter Planters

Deborah Scheblein
Welcome to Our Nest

Heathe Schutze
Fanciful Butterflies
Flowerpot Cover

Ruby Thacker
Lighthouse Frame

Laura Victory
Patriotism

Gina Woods
A Garden Is Fun
Can & Bottle Cozies
Garden Collage
Greenhouse
Fanciful Flights
Lemonade Straw Keeper
Quilts & Flowers
Tulips & Flags
Welcome Home Birdie
Whimsical Plant Pokes

Stitch Guide
Use the following diagrams to expand your plastic canvas stitching skills. For each diagram, bring needle up through canvas at the red number one and go back down through the canvas at the red number two. The second stitch is numbered in green. Always bring needle up through the canvas at odd numbers and take it back down through the canvas at the even numbers.

Background Stitches

The following stitches are used for filling in large areas of canvas. The Continental Stitch is the most commonly used stitch. Other stitches, such as the Condensed Mosaic and Scotch Stitch, fill in large areas of canvas more quickly than the Continental Stitch because their stitches cover a larger area of canvas.

Continental Stitch

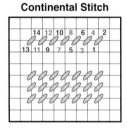

Condensed Mosaic

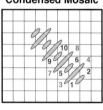

Alternating Continental

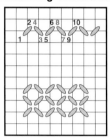

Cross Stitch

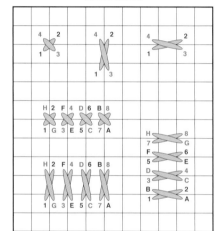

Long Stitch

Scotch Stitch

Slanting Gobelin

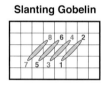

Embroidery Stitches

These stitches are worked on top of a stitched area to add detail to the project. Embroidery stitches are usually worked with one strand of yarn, several strands of pearl cotton or several strands of embroidery floss.

Lattice Stitch

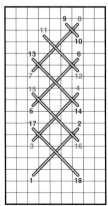

Chain Stitch

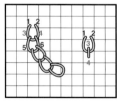

Straight Stitch

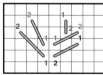

Fly Stitch

Couching

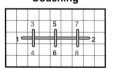

Running Stitch

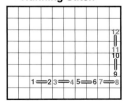

Backstitch

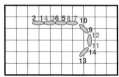

Embroidery Stitches

Lazy Daisy

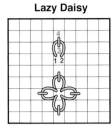

Bring yarn needle up through canvas, then back down in same hole, leaving a small loop. Then bring needle up inside loop; take needle back down through canvas on other side of loop.

French Knot

Bring needle up through canvas. Wrap yarn around needle 1 to 3 times, depending on desired size of knot; take needle back through canvas through same hole.

Loop Stitch/Turkey Loop Stitch

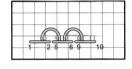

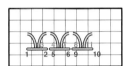

The top diagram shows this stitch left intact. This is an effective stitch for giving a project dimensional hair. The bottom diagram demonstrates the cut loop stitch. Because each stitch is anchored, cutting it will not cause the stitches to come out. A group of cut loop stitches gives a fluffy, soft look and feel to your project.

Specialty Stitches

The following stitches can be worked either on top of a previously stitched area or directly onto the canvas. Like the embroidery stitches, these, too, add wonderful detail and give your stitching additional interest and texture.

Satin Stitches

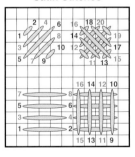

Smyrna Cross

Finishing Stitches

Overcast/Whipstitch

Overcasting and Whipstitching are used to finish the outer edges of the canvas. Overcasting is done to finish one edge at a time. Whipstitching is used to stitch two or more pieces of canvas together along an edge. For both Overcasting and Whipstitching, work one stitch in each hole along straight edges and inside corners, and two or three stitches in outside corners.

Lark's Head Knot

The Lark's Head Knot is used for a fringed edge or for attaching a hanging loop.

Buyer's Guide
When looking for a specific material, first check your local craft and retail stores. If you are unable to locate a product locally, contact the manufacturers listed below for the closest retail source in your area or a mail-order source.

Blumenthal Lansing Co.
(563) 538-3211
www.buttonsplus.com

Caron International
www.caron.com
public_relations@caron.com

Coats & Clark Inc.
(800) 648-1479
www.coatsandclark.com

Darice
Mail-order source:
Schrock's International
P.O. Box 538
Bolivar, OH 44612
(800) 426-4659

DMC Corp.
(800) 275-4117
www.dmc-usa.com

Lion Brand Yarn Co.
(800) 258-9276
www.lionbrand.com

One & Only Creations
(707) 255-8033
www.oneandonlycreations.com

Spinrite Inc.
(800) 265-2864
www.patonsyarns.com

Uniek
Mail-order source:
Annie's Attic
(800) 582-6643
www.anniesattic.com